SEASONS OF THE SPIRIT

SEASONS OF THE SPIRIT

by

SALLY COLEMAN
and
MARIA PORTER

 HAZELDEN®

Hazelden Educational Materials
Center City, Minnesota 55012-0176

ISBN: 1-56838-060-7

Editor's note:
Hazelden Educational Materials offers a variety of
information on chemical dependency and related
areas. Our publications do not necessarily represent
Hazelden's programs, nor do they officially speak for
any Twelve Step organization.

INTRODUCTION

At its kindest, age teaches us to make friends with ourselves and to tolerate and forgive others' differences. We are experiencing age now, not anticipating it as we did when we were children. We span several generations, those of us in mid-life. This is the time when our bodies have finished growing, and our minds and spirits can fully develop. As we grieve our losses and celebrate our victories we may find ourselves stopping to catch our breath, to reflect with wonder at how far we've come, and how many treasures we hold in our daily lives. That first Spring daffodil we always took for granted—if we ever noticed it at all—now fills us with joy. The sound of a loon fills us with profound comfort. A child's hand in ours feels like hearing a cosmic secret.

We hope this book will encourage you to see we are not alone in our shortcomings and regrets. As we step bravely out into the coming years, we deserve to enjoy them for the gift they are. Here we challenge you to be gentle with your humanity; to forgive the past and embrace the present; to live fully in each moment and step into each new day with a sense of purpose, wonder, and celebration.

—The authors

*There will never be another worry, another
anxiety, another care . . . strong enough to
alienate us from thy love . . . that is our
new year prayer.*

Preston Bradley

Today is the first day of our new year. We greet
this day as a special gift. It is a real opportunity to
recommit to positive expectations.

Pretend for a moment that this is the first day of
an experimental year. This is the year in which we will
leave *all* our worrying to God. Each day will challenge
our faith and trust. Each day will challenge us to act as
if we could do this, even if we don't believe we can.
Every morning in our quiet time we renew our experi-
ment. Today we are willing to give God all our worries, every last one. We are willing to let God remind
us of this all day long, whenever we forget our experi-
ment and take back our worries. We are willing, too,
to let go of having to remind ourselves. Reminders can
come from God through anyone or anything if we are
willing to see.

So will we move through our days, forgetting and
remembering. When we remember, however, whether
for a second or an hour, we are set free. God can bear
our every burden. God can enable and remind us to let
go. We need only ask.

*Today, let me trust God enough to completely let go
of my worries. Help me remember that God is still on
the job.*

January 2

*We are living in a fast-laned culture that is
losing touch with the rhythms of the seas,
the light of the stars, and the feel of the soil.*

Ben Hawkinson

Children in kindergarten resist learning to tell
time on a round-faced clock; they want to learn on a
digital watch. Are we, too, losing touch with the seasonal roundness of time? Our modern lives often speed
us into the technological tomorrow.

What kind of legacy do we wish to leave to our
children's children? We bear the traditions of yesterday, and today have an opportunity to speak to the
children of the things and times we have known. Were
we amazed at the miracle of radio? Did we gather
around it on a winter night? Did we play with marbles,
catch lightning bugs in jars, gallop on broomstick
horses, roller skate on the sidewalk? We have a lot
to tell.

But the memories themselves may not be as
important as our sharing them with the next generation. We need to pass on our living history as much as
our children need to hear it. They can only know who
they are by learning where they come from. We both
need the experience of coming together in this way.

*Today, let me make a point of remembering and shar-
ing my special memories with children.*

*To love is to give one's time. We never give
the impression that we care when we are in
a hurry.*

Paul Townier

A busy executive was confronted one day by an old
friend who said she felt sad because the executive never
seemed to have time for their friendship anymore.

The businesswoman thought a bit and realized she
had begun to put work first, instead of people. This
realization was so upsetting that she made a vow to
immediately slow down and let people back into her
life. Consciously, she worked each day to slow down
and concentrate when people spoke to her. She willed
herself to look at people and patiently gave them time.
Within three months, a sense of harmony and balance
had flowed back into her life.

At times we all rush past the needs of our loved
ones, forgetting *why* we are working so hard. But
slowing down is easy, and can bring our priorities back
in line. Time spent listening, caring, and sharing
enriches our lives. Suddenly we find life is richer,
more satisfying, more fulfilling. We find we love ourselves, and others, in a whole new way. We are
renewed.

Today, let me slow down to really hear people.

January 4

What is your glorious age?
A Chinese Question

In China, the aged are respected for their dignity, grace, and wisdom. Growing old is considered an honor.

What is your glorious age? Calling the aging process glorious goes against how we usually think about aging. What if we began viewing elders as wise and lucky? What if we celebrated rather than feared aging? What if we saw our older years as a gift, a blessing, rather than a burden to be endured?

What is your glorious age? To think of aging as glorious is to give the gift of attitude to ourselves and others. Considering all we have encountered along the road of life, can aging be anything but full of glory?

Today, let me begin to change my view of aging and see it as my reward, not as something to be endured.

Memory is what God gave us so we might have roses in December.

> *James M. Barrie*

Memories glitter like diamonds on a sunlit beach. Time makes poignant those pictures that anchor the corners of our memory. We each have snapshots that may light our long winter nights.

We may remember the shimmer of golden aspen leaves in October, the sweet tart taste of a McIntosh apple bought at a roadside stand, the old red blanket that found its way to all the football games, the familiar after-school clutter of gym shoes, school folders, damp bathroom floors, and the TV that never seemed to get turned off. We may remember having a case of the early morning grumps when it was time to get up for school, and the familiar sight of lunch money forgotten on the kitchen table.

With memory, there are no real losses in life. Those who are long gone burn as brightly as they did yesterday. We are still the five-year-old child, the teen, the young parent. In the storehouse of our minds, every pet, friend, and loved person is forever ours, to visit and revisit.

With memory, we are never alone, and need never be lonely.

Today, let me treasure the memories I make with those I love.

January 6

*I am willing to release the pattern within me
that is creating this condition.*

Louise Hay

We can create our own negative thought detector.
We can actually teach ourselves to sound an internal
alarm when we begin to get down on ourselves or others. Negative thinking is malignant. It can invade and
multiply in our lives, robbing us of our creative, healing energy.

Emotional stress and negativity can make us
physically sick. Awareness and respect for our own
power can be the beginning of loving and caring for
our whole person.

First we identify our troublemaking thoughts. We
may be so used to seeing only the negative—to actively
seeking it out—that we don't know where to begin to
cultivate a positive attitude. Do we consider life a good
or a bad thing? Do we feel lovable? Do we expect the
worst or the best from people and events? How can we
develop a more optimistic view of ourselves and the
world?

Developing the awareness necessary for change
takes a commitment. A nightly review of our thinking
pattern may be a good place to begin. The more aware
we become, the greater power we will have to change
our lives from negative to positive.

*Today, let me take the time to be aware of my daily
thinking patterns.*

*If you genuinely love or at least send kind
thoughts to a thing, it will change before
your eyes.*

      John and Lyn St. Clair Thomas

Work takes up the majority of our time and we deserve to leave the office happy. We may have to learn to adjust our attitudes and tolerate people who are very different. We might do everything in our power to be assertive and negotiate differences, but in the end we are usually stuck with a few situations and people who will test our patience.

How will we act at work? What kind of mental attitude will we display? Are we going to hold on to resentment and self-pity regarding people and situations beyond our control? Or will we decide to be productive, positive, and happy in spite of it all?

Learning to let go of our resentments and even wishing difficult people well can help ease our stress and free us from the pull of negative energy, which drags us down. Work can become a healthier, happier place to spend our days when we change our attitude and expectations.

Today, let me realize that I am the master of my own fate and mental attitude and I can determine what kind of day I will have at work.

January 8

I never give them hell. I just tell the truth and they think it is hell.

Harry S Truman

How difficult it is, sometimes, to say what we are truly thinking. We have trouble talking straight because we don't want to hurt others, or we don't want to be disliked. But for others to trust us, and for us to be trustworthy, we must be forthright. We must learn to talk straight.

When we fear telling the truth, it's often because our people-pleasing insecurities are intense; we try hard to hurt no one, and as a result the truth is lost and everyone is hurt. When we tangle ourselves in stories and lies, we forget the hurtful consequences to others and to our own integrity.

Other times we don't care. We find ourselves so detached and emotionally distant that we don't care enough to make the effort to talk straight. Yet in our hearts we know that healthy living relationships thrive on the simplicity of truth.

Whatever our reasons, we know by now that the truth sets us free. Telling the truth can become a habit that lets us sleep in peace and live with a clean conscience.

Today, let me strive for honesty and directness in my speech.

*It is eternally tragic
that which is magic
will be killed at the end
of the glorious chase.*

John Denver

Seals and whales are hunted and slaughtered to make coats and perfumes. We and our planet suffer the loss. Part of our gift to life as we grow in health can be a greater awareness of life's interconnectedness, and a greater reverence for the earth and for life in all its forms. To revere the earth is to revere ourselves.

But what can one person do to protect life on our planet? We can recognize our power—we can realize that each of us has a voice, and voices joining together can bring powerful changes.

As we open our eyes to living, we may feel a need to reciprocate some of the gifts we've been given. More and more we realize that every human being is connected, one to the other. As we come to value all life more and more we are willing to preserve and protect it.

Today, let me raise my voice for what I believe to be right. Help me remember that we all share the same sky, and that we are responsible to each other.

January 10

Dreams are like the rudder of a ship setting sail. The rudder may be small and unseen, but it controls the ship's course.

      Kim Woo-choong

If in our youth we were discouraged from daydreaming because it meant we were idle or lazy, now let us consider the value of allowing the daydreams to resurface.

Deep within us are desires, talents, and goals that have been dormant for years. Daydreams can let these rise up into the light. Some we may examine and discard; in others we may find real treasures, long forgotten, that still hold promise.

Dreams can be encouraged to merge with our middle-age reality. We may find a new direction, a long-forgotten goal, or insight into our hidden selves. Our dreams may inspire a change in our life course that can bring untold joy for the rest of our lives.

Today, let me know my daydreams can be significant, not frivolous.

*I know well that hate is a consuming fire,
poisoning every part of us, yet there are
times when it has to be met, for some
degree of it is as cleansing as fire.*

Florida Scott-Maxwell

Do we see anger as only destructive? Or do we accept anger as a feeling, a signal that something is wrong? Anger as a way of life is counterproductive, it can warp the spirit. Yet anger, when unexpressed, erupts as rage or festers into resentment, causing illness in body and mind.

Anger expressed directly is a call to action, to change. It motivates us instantly. Like a surgeon's knife, it is often the only way to cut through our need to please others. For some of us, only the energy of anger can help us be assertive enough to state our needs and get those needs met. Only the pain of anger can tell us who we really are and help us change.

Today, let me see the value of anger and the need for change it signals.

January 12

*We cannot give to any man without giving
to every man.*

Maurice Francois

Migrating geese fly in a V formation to save energy. In the flying wedge, each bird gets a lift from the current left by the bird ahead. This makes flying easier for all except the leader. During a migration, geese take turns in the lead position so no one bird must bear the difficulty alone.

Geese instinctively seem to understand the need for cooperation and community in living together. We may learn the value of shared effort and support from their simple cooperative spirit.

Learning to live in peace and harmony with our fellows is the ultimate task of maturity and wisdom. A willingness to share the burdens of life brings us a new sense of belonging, of being part of the universe. Understanding that what happens to you also happens to me is the foundation of global responsibility and love.

Today, let me treat each person I meet as I would like to be treated.

*Emptiness is beautiful because it has the
capacity to be everything.*
    Lee Chang

In the East an empty rice bowl is a symbol of
prosperity. Asians see it as a gift. A full rice bowl is of
no further use because we can no longer choose what
goes into it.

In the East emptiness is valued far more than fullness. In the simplicity of emptiness lies potentially
everything but especially peace and tranquility.

In our rush to become full we may lose touch with
the healing energy of simplicity and quiet. Full of anxiety, we rush about, productive and efficient. We may
get a lot accomplished, but what happens to our deeper
spiritual needs, which are best met when we slow
down, when we turn away from our usual distractions?

When we keep our rice bowls full to overbrim-
ming, there is no room for simplicity, for the emptiness out of which serenity and healing energy arise.

*Today, let me slow down and take the time to empty
out the clutter of my mind.*

January 14

Time (and personal energy) is the coin of your life. It is the only coin you have. Be careful lest someone else spend it for you.

Carl Sandburg

Without energy, we have little zest for living and loving. Personal energy is the life force that lets us be productive, joyous, and involved in activity and recreation.

Some of us have acted as if we had a limitless supply of energy. We believed we could constantly respond to everyone and everything, and told ourselves we would take care of our own needs tomorrow.

But tomorrow never made its way into today. Burning our candle at both ends only left us exhausted and depressed. After years of such outward focusing, we lost the ability to identify and meet our needs.

In mid-life, one of our most important tasks may be the journey we make back to ourselves. Coming to know ourselves, we learn to listen to the messages sent by our minds, hearts, and bodies. We learn to give time and thought to our own needs. In this way we approach health and serenity.

Today, let me understand that to truly give to others, I must first fill up my own personal storehouse.

*Meditation is as simple and easy as we
allow it to be.*

> *Sam Friend*

A certain Zen teacher began each day at dawn with a walk in his garden. Every morning he would look for the most perfect flower. Having found his blossom for the day, he would meditate on its beauty and wholeness. That flower helped set his internal pace and attitude for the day.

What symbol or image do we find most beautiful or comforting? What would happen to the rhythm of our day if we began each morning with the actual or imagined company of this symbol as our spiritual guide? Shutting out the rest of the world to meditate is a gift we can give ourselves.

Thirty days of consistent meditation can elicit positive change in our lives. The simpler the meditation—the fewer the rules or guidelines—the better. If we take the time to sit still, breathe easily, and focus on something comforting, our body and spirit will slow down and teach us how to be spiritually filled.

Today, let me begin treating myself to a regular quiet time.

January 16

How do I love thee?
Let me count the ways . . .
Elizabeth Barrett Browning

We all desire to love and be loved. We would like the best parts of ourselves to be brought forth by love. Our sadness is deep when love doesn't mirror our goodness and caring. When we act with insensitivity toward our beloved, we disappoint ourselves as well as the other.

Why is it so hard to be loving in some relationships? When our desire is to love, why do we strike out in anger? Why do our partners become dumping grounds for our accumulation of life's pain?

Sometimes we may expect to be cared for without caring in return. Some days we expect too much, that our loved ones can and will "make it better." But in mid-life we're learning that in good relationships we get what we give. Trust, patience, compassion, and respect are returned in kind. We're learning that we are not always perfect, and neither is our partner. We're learning to overlook the bad, and count the ways we love.

Today, let me cherish my loved ones.

Good, to forgive; Best, to forget!
Robert Browning

Liberation from crippling parental guilt begins when we accept the fact that our family isn't like a TV sit-com. Many of us grew up with the myth of the consistently good and wise parents whose perfect children become doctors, dentists, and Supreme Court judges.

Being a parent teaches us about humanness and limitations, ours and our children's. As we make poor decisions and watch our offspring do the same we have a choice. We can accept that it is possible and wise to love others for whom they are today because we're all doing the best we can, or we can continue tilting at windmills by expecting the impossible from ourselves and our families.

This doesn't mean we forsake our values and ideals. It means we learn to lighten up, roll with the punches, and take off our judge's robes, so we may better experience life. We can learn to forgive and forget, to love ourselves and our children just as we are.

Today, let me forgive and accept myself for being an imperfect parent.

January 18

Say I'm weary, say I'm sad,
Say that health and wealth have missed me,
Say I'm growing old, but add,
Jenny kissed me.

James Henry Leigh Hunt

Certain memories, like beacon lights, brighten up the rooms of our mind. Learning to cherish them is a gift of the years. All of our senses are enlivened by beauties from the past.

We drive through tall pine trees on a sun-speckled day, and again we are seven, on our way to summer camp. We hold a baby, and the smell of powder takes us back to our children when they were babies, to the feel of their little bodies in our arms. A certain melody we loved thirty years ago reminds us of a moment so pure and magic it still makes our breath catch.

Treasures are sprinkled throughout our years. They affirm our capacity to continue to love and build tomorrow's memories.

Today we rejoice anew in the smell of cinnamon baked apples in autumn and summer garden roses. Church bells, crickets, foghorns, and November winds bring back faces and events. Memory keeps the past alive and can redeem the present.

Today, let me build a joyful memory.

Optimism is grace in action.

Sam Friend

An optimist is one who falls from a 20-story building and at every story shouts, "I'm all right so far." Optimism is a gift we can pass on to others. We have a choice about how we view our world, and each morning choose how we will live our day. We can choose to focus on negatives, or we can choose to expect the best for the next 24 hours. We are generally as happy as we make up our minds to be.

There is great power in positive thinking. When we feel frightened about something in the day ahead, we can practice visualization. We can visually rehearse the fearful event, picturing ourselves in the best possible light. What would we like to have happen? How best might the situation turn out? Then we can practice seeing those positive results and seeing ourselves as confident, happy, and full of energy.

We don't have to be paralyzed by fear. We can learn to confront terror and work it through. Visualizations can disarm our fears. They can help us approach the day and our lives more positively.

Today, let me choose to believe that I am exactly where I am supposed to be. Never let me forget that God's plan for me is good.

January 20

Mom died when I was sixty and I felt like an orphan.

Fred Fresard

No matter how old we are, we may feel like lost children when our parents die. Now we are becoming the older generation, the caretakers. The death of a parent puts us in touch with our own mortality. As we were growing up, our parents seemed so old, and we felt like we would live forever in our youth. The day we are no longer someone's child is the day we experience a new kind of reality. A part of us feels orphaned and abandoned. We realize that the clock of our lives can't be stopped. We find ourselves face-to-face with the cycle of living and dying that we have shared with our ancestors since the beginning of time.

At first we may try to wait out our pain, but grief has a long memory. There is no cure for feelings of loss. Experiencing the death of a parent is a milestone in growing up. When we face and express our childhood fears about the death of our parents, we have more room for life. Freedom from this fear and acceptance of our own mortality enlarge our perspective. When we accept, finally, just how limited we are, we find ourselves availed of compassion and serenity whose source is unlimited.

Today, let me give myself all the time I need to completely grieve the deaths of my parents.

*Work addiction is the great robber of time,
love and peace of mind.*

John Forest

When our ambitions take over, we can lose sight
of our priorities. When work becomes the most important thing in our life, we quickly get off balance. Work
addiction, like other addictions, may be a problem if
our work is continually disrupting or spilling over into
other arenas of our life.

Is our physical or emotional health affected by our
work? Is work the primary way we validate our self-
worth? Has our work become more important than our
relationships? Do we find it harder to take time off
from work, or to leave work at the office? Have our
family and friends complained that we don't spend
enough time with them?

To regain our balance, we can ask others about
their feelings. Change begins with an honest appraisal
of our work life and how it affects ourself and others.
But we can change, we can learn to find balance in our
lives. And in changing, we can find a whole new world
opening up to us, a world we were too busy to enjoy.
We become closer to our loved ones, and open to the
beauty of the world around us. Our lives can have a
rich new meaning.

*Today, let me have the willingness to slow down and
catch up with the reality of how I spend my time.*

January 22

*I realized that not even when my children
were babies had I ever felt such a rush of
tenderness toward another person as the
first time I noticed the bald circle that had
begun at the back of my husband's head.*

Judith Wax

Married love is like a boat that has survived
stormy seas. Over the years it collects barnacles that
need to be removed to keep it upright.

Married love consists of big events and small
moments of tenderness that are woven into the fabric
of our days. It is sitting across the same table and passing the same cream pitcher for thousands of mornings.
It is fighting the same old fights, having no resolution,
but being willing to love each other anyway.

Married love is years of shared worries about
babies, money, illness, teenagers, and the future. For
some, it is learning the art of negotiating differences
and mending fences. It is learning to say, "I'm sorry,"
when we are at fault, and learning not to say,
"I'm sorry," when it is not our fault. It is learning the
difference.

Married love usually turns out to be different
from what we had planned, but it is one unique bond
with another human. There is great comfort in knowing our life has been witnessed, shared, and loved by
another.

*Today, let me be grateful for the ups and downs in my
marriage; they are teaching me about myself.*

*My own pain and worry will diminish in
proportion to my willingness to be there
for others.*

Jerome Smith

A teacher described her vision of heaven and hell
to her students. Hell, she said, was a room with a
round table at which six people were seated. Each had
a bowl of food and a spoon, but because the spoons
they held were longer than their arms all were slowly
starving. They couldn't feed themselves.

Heaven, the teacher said, was the same: the room,
the round table, six people sitting with long spoons in
their hands. In this vision, however, the people were
smiling, joyful, and full of health. They were using
the long spoons to feed each other.

Today, let me know that when I give, I am given to.

We will have to let go of so much of what we hoped we could do for our children. And, of course, we will have to let go of our children, too.

Judith Viorst

Separating from our children is sweet sadness. For so long we have traveled the same path, but now we are asked to let go, realizing we will never again be needed in quite the same way. We turn them over to a world filled with peril and pain. A part of us still feels they will be unsafe without our protection.

A stronger belief in the goodness and hope of life can sustain us during this hard time. We often feel saddened by our children's leaving. There may be so much more we wanted to give before they left.

We grieve over the loss of giving less than we'd hoped, and we grieve over our imperfections as parents. But we can survive. One day soon the sun will shine again and we'll rediscover our own lives. Now, we can be friends with our children and find a whole new and rewarding relationship with these lovable, fascinating new adults.

Today, let me be gentle with my shortcomings as a parent. Help me focus on the good I've brought into their lives.

*People are living with a runaway sense of
the clock and the result is time sickness.*

Larry Dossey

To beat the clock on the wall, we speed up our internal clocks and race our bodies and emotions to produce, produce, produce. Rigid attitudes about productivity and the pushing of time can make us vulnerable to stress and even illness. When the clock takes over in our lives, we become its stressed-out servant.

For those of us afflicted by this "busy sickness" it is hard to slow down and relax. We may feel anxiety when we try to moderate our pace and do less. Unstructured free time can be terrifying when we are used to running on a daily speed track.

Constant hurrying can be used to escape and anesthetize our real feelings. Many people actually get high on the charged-up feeling of activity and more activity.

But we can change. Spending a few quiet minutes each morning can help us focus on our priorities and need for balance. When we feel ourselves pressured, we can take a break, go for a walk, or just sit a moment and relax.

Letting go of the pressure of time can open up a fresh new way to live, today and every day.

*Today, let me slow down long enough to discover I
actually need to slow down.*

January 26

God is the friend of silence. Trees, flowers,
grass grow in silence. See the stars, moon
and sun, how they move in silence.

Mother Teresa

God has given us a garden of silence where we can go to rest. Silence is a friend we can sit with when we are overflowing with life and need peace. The most amazing gifts come to us in and through our quiet times. In silence we touch hands with the sacred. Having thus known its power to restore us, we will know it is a privilege worth fighting for every day.

Silence allows us to slow down long enough to reaffirm our power, and refill our sources of energy. It gives us the courage to return, strengthened, to the arena of life. Silence allows us to see the beauty and tragedy of life from a position of serene distance.

Finding the comfort of silence takes time and commitment. But in time we can learn to relax and accept the healing gifts silence brings.

Today, let me welcome silence into my life.

Faith, hope, and love and the greatest of these is love.

> *Cor. 13:13*

An American Folk tale tells of an elderly grandmother who is spending her final years in the home of her daughter. Occasionally she would break a dish and finally her daughter gave her a wooden bowl and said she was to eat only out of that bowl. The youngest child and granddaughter asked her mother why her grandmother was eating out of a wooden bowl when the rest of the family had nice glass bowls. "Because she is old," was the reply. The youngest child thought for a moment and said, "You must save the wooden bowl when grandmother dies." "Why?" asked her mother. Her child quietly answered, "For when you are old."

In mid-life, we are challenged to begin thinking about our values and how they affect the aging process of ourselves and those we love. How do we want to be treated when we're old? How will we treat the senior adults in our lives? Are our reactions based on love or fear?

We can choose to grow into our tomorrows reflecting the person we wish to be.

Today, let me believe that the loving price of dignity is worth an occasional broken dish or extra effort.

January 28

Is the universe friendly?
    Albert Einstein

Choosing to live asks us to be willing to believe in the basic goodness of life. If we find we still believe the universe is not friendly, we are challenged to "act as if," or "fake it till we make it."

When we start with the premise that the world is out to get us, we will focus on and attract negative people, places, and events. What a burden for us to carry and for others to feel. Life gives back pretty much what we put into it, and negativity is a boomerang that finds its way home.

But when we learn to trust the world to be a friendly place, we focus on the good around us. Soon we feel happier, more loving and serene.

A regular internal housecleaning is often needed to sweep out the dust of negativity that can settle on our days. And when we question our negative attitudes we can ask ourselves, "What's the other side of the coin?" There is always another side. Once we see this, we can see that it is up to us to choose which one we look at. The positive or the negative. What a delight to approach a new day grounded in the belief that good things will come our way.

Today, let me start out expecting that my positive attitude will attract good things.

*Finally, I stand before the Lord and find to
my surprise that he considers me a treasure.*

Anthony de Mello

We are all treasures, enduring survivors, bright,
beautiful, and full of goodness. We are farmers, mer-
chants, and artists who delight in our toil, craft, and
product. We are singers of song and creators of love
poems who write by the light of a desert full of stars.
We deserve to dance under the sun and play in night-
time seas. We are unique in creation, beautiful gifts
made from God's hand.

We are tall, short, freckled, smooth, white, black,
and brown. We are the more lovely for our imperfections. We are the builders of the next generations and
have given our best grace and wisdom. We are also the
humanness of mistakes.

We are more than we imagine. We are connected
through our love and tears to one another. We are all
equal, and worthy of love, freedom, and fellowship.
We are beautiful in this moment, exactly as we are
today.

Today, let me treat myself as the treasure that I am.

January 30

I was seventy-seven, come August. I shall shortly be losing my bloom.

Dorothy Parker

We are as young as we feel. It has been said that youth is a state of mind. Active involvement in life keeps us full of zest. We have all met senior adults who were a delight to know. They seem to have the best of both worlds: the vitality of youth and the wisdom of years. How did they get that way?

The middle years set the stage for the kind of people we will be in our seventies and eighties. Today is the only day to begin planning for a positive retirement attitude. We can ask ourselves questions: In what ideal condition I would like my attitude to be someday? What kind of attitude do I want to develop about the world? Do I want to live with gratitude and positive expectations?

We plant the seeds of our future today. Today we are challenged to believe we can think our way into positive living and experiencing. We can learn to wear rose-colored glasses again, and keep blooming in all the years to come.

Today, let me believe that my positive attitude will keep my life blooming.

It is true love because he is willing to wear unironed undershirts out of respect for the fact that I am philosophically opposed to ironing.

Judith Viorst

Power struggles in relationships are like TNT—they do nothing but cause damage. Love is a give-and-take arrangement, and often we give more than we take.

But truly caring for someone's welfare means being willing to give one hundred percent on some days. In good relationships, there are no winners and losers, just winners. We learn to make allowances for our loved one, and each time we swallow our ego and put the cap back on the toothpaste instead of complaining, we win a victory for love.

Happy love is a two-way street of give and take, forgive and forget. Nursed hurt feelings, long memories, and power struggles do not nourish happy love.

Love grows best when we accept differences without forcing change and wish our beloved's personal dreams to come true.

Today, let me be grateful for the opportunity to practice tolerance in my give-and-take love relationship.

February 1

*The more we drink from the rivers of spiri-
tuality, the more we thirst.*

Ali Moreno

As we throw off the burdens of our youth we are
becoming more aware of a deep yearning for our own
version of God. In describing this yearning, a very
busy woman in a religious order said, "I crave my time
with Him."

There are no rules about how our spiritual needs
can be met. We may find this peace in a boat, deeply
aware of the marvels of water and wind, or on our
hands and knees weeding the flower garden. Walking,
sitting still, running, or meditating are ways we may
get that "at one" feeling. It is for each of us to discover
our own path and our own Higher Power.

The needs of our spirit can serve as an accurate
barometer for the rest of our lives. When we regularly
feed the soul, we can count on the rest of us being in
balance.

*Today, let me find a way to meet my need for spiritual
nourishment.*

*Thousands of gifts, continually returning
to us.*

Garrison Keillor

To feel awe is to be touched by the wonder of
things. Awe asks that we remain open, be childlike,
and expect daily miracles in our lives. Awe is circular
and never-ending, it comes with the seasons and is
found in small shared moments and in solitude. It is in
the perfect form of a daffodil and the howling winds of
a coastal winter storm. It is in that moment when the
bride lets go of her father's arm. It is also in colors and
sounds, and in the smells of pine, vanilla, mimosa,
and oceanfront towns.

We can feel awe in the almost perfect clarity of
evening light on country fields. Awe is found in shared
sexuality and the amazement of discovering a spiritual
connection with another human being.

Awe is the same and different for each of us. As
long as we are aware of the world around us, we
never end.

Today, let me experience awe.

February 3

When we build our life foundation out of love,
we will always have a home to return to.

Sam Friend

St. Augustine had one single moral principle: "Love and do what you want." If we were to truly understand the meaning of love, we would live life to the fullest while stepping softly around the hearts of others.

When we get up in the morning and dedicate our day to love, we lay a foundation for joy and fellowship with ourselves, family, and friends.

To connect with love, we can ask ourselves one question throughout the day: "Is what I'm doing loving to myself and others?" Love-based actions bring us freedom from fear. The true lovers of life are easy to recognize. They laugh freely and listen to others with an open, non-judgmental face. Rooms seem to get brighter when they walk in. Lovers of life also sleep well at night, grateful for the privilege of loving another day.

Today, let me embrace all of life with love in my heart.

*. . . we cannot live in the afternoon of life
according to the program of life's morning.
For what in the morning was true, will at
evening have become a lie.*

    C.G. Jung

Changing the way we live, the way we see ourselves and the world, is no easy trick. Mid-life challenges us to review our old beliefs and attitudes. Like a
trunk full of old clothes, we rummage through our lives
trying to decide what to keep and what to give away.

Our past life is a treasure box full of possible attitudes and beliefs. When we shop through all these possibilities, we are the masters of our fate. We can choose
the kind of attitudes we want to have, and be the people
we want to be for the second half of our lives.

Do we want to get rid of some old jealousy
because it doesn't seem to fit right any more? What
about our critical comments—do they wear well on
ourselves and others? Perhaps a little tolerance and
forgiveness will better complement the style we'd like
to live in today. Making changes now is not always
easy. It requires honesty and attention and commitment. Mid-life can be a time of great purpose,
renewal, and change if we open ourselves to new ideas
and make a commitment to making at least a little progress each day toward who we want to be.

*Today, let me take the best from my wardrobe of life
and discard the rest.*

February 5

Something that is yours forever is never precious.

Chaim Potok

All human life is in transition. As life gives and takes, we grow to cherish the gifts we are given. We have to remember a special look on our baby daughter's face when she was two; we never quite re-capture that look unless we have a photo, but we try. The deep-felt warmth of a tight hug after a long absence fills another memory room in our heart. Then there was the night we spent drinking hot chocolate and singing old songs with friends. And a camping trip with a spectacular sunset. Holding the beauty of these moments in our hearts, we are filled with an abundance of joy, even when the moment is long ago.

But learning to cherish the past is not what our lives are for. We are here to cherish the present. We know now that nothing stays the same. Children grow up and go off into their own lives. We move to different neighborhoods and leave friends behind. Often, the sports we once played are part of the past. Our duty today is to seize the moment, live it fully, and let it go so we can seize the next.

Today, let me embrace change with gratitude, knowing I will never really lose the joys of today.

To the extent that we want something from someone, to that exact degree we will be in pain. For it is desire that brings pain.
Joan Walsh Anglund

Expecting our children to make us happy will frustrate and disappoint us. Sometimes we feel we deserve to be paid back, and who owes us more than the children we sacrificed for? We may expect them to appreciate us, anticipate our needs, and fill the empty spots in our days.

But children involved in their own lives are independent, busy, and achievement-oriented. They will sometimes be there for us in crisis, but in day-to-day living they pretty much go their own way. This is not only their right, it is necessary to the fulfillment of their own destinies. The harder we try to hang on, the harder they will pull away. Our final task as parents is to accept the reality that it is good and healthy for our children to leave us.

Now, we have a choice. We can feel sorry for ourselves, or grieve and let go of expectations. In letting go, we can begin to make a new life for ourselves.

Today, let me believe that wings are the best gift I can give to my children.

February 7

God has still a work for me to do.
John Henry Newman

A strong inner voice on a long train ride in 1946 led a nun in her mid-thirties to choose a plan for the second half of her life. Mother Teresa chose to give up the comforts and familiarity of home because she felt called to go out into the streets of Calcutta to minister to the poorest of the poor. She respected the wisdom of her intuition and took the risk of following the uncertain path.

The decision to try something more or take a new direction may come to us as we age. The alternatives we now face in life may be very different from those we've known. Some are safe paths, and others might be unknown. We often feel impelled to travel the uncertain path as a persistent inner voice says, "Do it, it feels right! Take the chance."

During the first half of our lives, we gained knowledge, security, and courage. Now, we can put those tools to use to find a new way to live and to live it. As we listen to ourselves, we will find what we need.

Today, let me get to know myself well enough to hear the yearning voice of my heart.

*Anyone who takes the safe road is as good
as dead.*

      C.G. Jung

A famous author finished writing a novel at three
in the morning. Then he went around and woke up his
small children, sat them on the mantelpiece, and
played Mozart for them in celebration.

Celebrating life often challenges us to forget about
the way we look to others. Trusting ourselves enough
to respond spontaneously is great fun and the purest
way to share our feelings with others.

The longer we live the more we can risk being naturally outrageous. Who do we really need to please
except ourselves? We may sing at the top of our lungs,
wear orange socks with purple pants, dye our hair
pink, or save money each month to climb Mount Kili-
manjaro. We don't have to be young to act young.
Youth is a state of mind. It's the ability to firmly plant
our feet on the earth and claim our right to be the person we want to be.

Today, let me give free rein to my celebration of life.

February 9

*What paralyzes life is the failure to believe
and the failure to dare.*

Pierre Teilhard de Chardin

We open the doors to life when we dare to love others. When we expose our hearts to caring, we must necessarily be vulnerable and open. And by keeping our hearts open to giving love, we become available to receive it.

In matters of the heart, life may have brought us pain as well as joys. Few of us survive the years without being hurt at some time or other in love relationships.

There is a story of a woman who had her heart broken nine times but she continued to be open to love despite her pain. A good friend asked her how she could have the courage to keep believing in the possibility of finding a good love relationship. She replied, "Love has been my teacher in the school of life. It's my time to get an 'A,' and I won't quit right before graduation."

We can all keep striving to risk pain in order to gain happiness. If we only look, we will find the courage we need to continue in our own hearts.

Today, let me believe love will find me.

*When did the boys I once clung to start
losing their hair?*

      Judith Viorst

How did we get to be middle-aged on the outside when we still feel like riding merry-go-rounds on the inside? When did we start getting short, proper hair-cuts, longing for the longer style we once loved to swing and brush back? How long since we considered catching a firefly in a jar or running barefoot through summer grass?

Where has time gone? Can the mounting years on our calendar be real? What about all the things we dreamed of doing? What about the fairy tales that never came true? When we were in our twenties, we felt we would be young forever. We magically believed that getting old was for our parents and other people. Unwrinkled, we embraced youth feeling we'd always be someone else's children.

Time seems to catch up with a bang! Suddenly we find ourselves sitting on the other side of the line, unprepared for gravity's pull and the fact of our own mortality.

But it's never too late to enjoy life. The world is still a wondrous parade, and we can join it. We've all known very youthful grandparents—and very "old" teenagers. We can live long and happily, loving our-selves and others. Mid-life can be a new beginning, rather than an end.

Today, let me enjoy one wonderful old memory and one bright thought for the future.

February 11

It is virtually impossible to feel guilty and
hopeful at the same time.

Julius Segal

Guilt and hope aren't compatible because they have opposite energy needs. Hope is the positive uplifting of the spirit; guilt is a slow spiral into depression.

We can choose to look at life from the position of winner or victim. Guilt is a fact of our imperfect human life. How we deal with guilt dictates who we are. We can sit around in its muck, or name it, claim it, and let it go.

Survivors are hope-based people who make lemonade when life gives them lemons. When we stay rooted in guilt we rob ourselves of the privilege of dealing with our problems.

Hope is what keeps us going in the most difficult of circumstances. It can heal illness and mend hurt relationships. Hope is the best lifesaver we can have in the world of today and it is always available to us because it's innate to the human heart. When we can't find it ourselves, a friend can help if we only ask, and just by asking, we are acting on hope.

Today, let me make hope my best resource.

*It often happens that I wake up at night and
begin to think about a serious problem and
decide I must tell the Pope about it. Then I
wake up completely and remember that I am
the Pope.*

Pope John XXIII

Decisions need not frighten us if we develop an
awareness of our purpose in life. What kind of person
are we? What are the deep values, visions, and goals
we have chosen for our lives?

When we become clear about who we are, we
find it easier to make decisions. We can ask ourselves,
"Does this decision fit with my life's purpose? Will it
add to the harmony of my life? Does it contribute to
my peace of mind, or rob me of energy?"

It has been said that the three tasks of humans are
to work, to love, and to decide. Many of us love well
and work productively but are afraid to go out on the
limb of decision-making. To avoid choosing, we may
even push others into deciding for us.

Trusting anew in our ability to risk making decisions gives us our integrity and freedom. Letting go of
"decision paralysis" is often the stepping-stone that
leads us to possible life changes.

*Today, let me not be afraid to claim my rightful power
as a decision-maker in my own life.*

February 13

*And the fine sun of fifty saw him dying and
alone. Just a man who spent all his life
hoping once to soar.*
Rod McKuen

Do we put off our dreams until tomorrow, thinking we'll start really living when the kids are grown, the mortgage is paid off, when we retire, when we finally take that trip to Bermuda?

Do we imagine that life will be perfect when we have time to paint water colors, when work isn't so busy, when we have enough money in the bank, when we leave the city and move to the shore, or when we get ourselves into better physical shape?

Is there a "right time" to really enjoy life and live our dreams? A wise woman decided to begin following her dreams at age forty. She listed fifty dreams and made a commitment to make one dream come true each year. Today she is seventy-five. She is thirty-five dreams lighter and a very happy, alive woman.

We can follow her example and start living today. Every new day brings us a chance to fulfill a dream, to enjoy this twenty-four hours while it's still ours.

Today, let me begin living my dreams instead of putting them off until some distant tomorrow.

Love for the joy of loving, and not for the offerings of someone else's heart.

Marlene Dietrich

Freely-given, non-possessive love enriches us with health. Jealous, controlling love causes us to feel confused, depressed, and guilty. When we can't accept others as they are, when we are suspicious and wary, we find ourselves on a terrible merry-go-round. When things are not perfect, we examine our actions and wonder what we did wrong or blame someone else for what we feel they did wrong.

There are no winners when our love relationship is based on fear, power, and control. Then we are always fearful, always vigilant, never trusting that it's safe to stand still and be who we are.

When it's healthy, love adds to our life, it doesn't deplete us. We wake up in the morning full of hope instead of dread. We trust ourselves to be worthy of love, and trust others to love us. We give ourselves and others the benefit of the doubt. We ask rather than interrogate. We request rather than demand.

Healthy love brings us peace and contentment and a feeling of oneness with the world and with God.

Today, let me examine the health of my relationships.

February 15

Trust is not a promise that good will auto-matically come, but that something good is somehow already present.

Christina Baldwin

Trust is learning to believe in our internal nudges. It is following the small daily miracles of life. When we are faced with two choices, we will always be shown which direction is best for us, if we have the patience to get quiet, to wait, and listen to our intuition.

Today we are being led in the path that is just right for us. We are exactly where we need to be in our life today. Difficult situations and people are teachers who challenge us to learn new truths about ourselves.

We know the answers to all the problems we have today. We carry the decision that is best for us inside our hearts. We need only to get quiet and listen for our right direction.

Today, let me know that no decision is too difficult to make when I trust, quiet down, and listen to my intuition.

*Death is stingless indeed, and as beautiful
as life . . . the grave has no victory, for it
never fights. All is divine harmony.*
　　　　John Muir

Nature teaches us about the harmonious, purposeful balance in life and death. There is a deep com-
munion in all living and growing things. A cycle of
endings and beginnings, planting and harvesting,
springs and falls. Our fear of death is born of our
resistance to that natural order and flow of life. We forget our place in a bigger picture and view death as an
unnatural act or attack. We may even let our fear of
death rob us of our joy today.

Dr. Elizabeth Kubler-Ross speaks of death as a
natural "transition" into beauty and harmony. She
feels that death is really a "birth-day." In studies of
near-death experiences, there are countless stories told
of an experience so joyous that its beauty is impossible
to describe.

Perhaps death is merely a doorway into a love-
filled tomorrow. We walk to the door when the time is
right, and it will open for us into peace beyond our
understanding.

Today, let me enjoy my life without fear.

February 17

The pace with which you begin the day,
is the pace you will maintain throughout
the day.

Eknath Easwaran

There is a saying in India that if you skip one day's meditation, it takes seven days to catch up. Morning meditation and quiet time is our daily "soul food." It sets the course of our day and aims us in the right direction. We can use morning as a time of renewal, centering, and new beginnings, a time to gently let go of yesterday and create an attitude of positive expectation for the new day.

Days that begin with hurried neglect of our spiritual needs are not going to be healthy. Giving ourselves the gift of a morning prayer time sets a gentle pace for a balanced day. Tea, sunshine, birds, and new light are the gifts we give ourselves in our morning prayers and meditation.

Instead of feeling hurried and out of balance, we can start each morning with serenity. Meditation frees us from worry and grants us peace to sustain our hearts the whole day.

Today, let me renew my commitments to make my spiritual well-being a priority.

*Somehow I learned how to listen to the
sound of the sun going down.*

    John Denver

Our Higher Power is a friend who yearns for us to
sit down and pour out our hearts. We will always hear
an answer when we take the time to listen.

Meditation and quiet times bring us the time to
listen. As we slow down our external pace, our internal spaces open up to the needs of our spirit and a healing channel of energy flows in and around us.

Our spiritual life doesn't need to be complicated
or fancy. Simplicity is the key word of the spirit. When
we sit with our Higher Power, we don't have to be anyone except ourselves. We can take our mask off and
just be ourselves. Our Higher Power finds us totally
lovable and right, exactly as we are in each moment.

*Today, let me listen for the voice of my Higher Power in
my life.*

February 19

Our noses become so clogged by pollution, cigarettes, deodorants, our lungs so constricted by shallow, rapid breathing that we lose the scent of life.

>   *Sam Keen*

When is the last time we laid out under the stars or in a stand of pines? Do we remember what it feels like to look up at the universe and ponder infinity? Have we forgotten the pure clean smell of the pine needles that delights our senses? How long has it been since we walked barefoot in the grass or mud? Was there a recent time when we laid in the sand by the sea and felt our wet body mold into the nestling shore?

And what of birds and butterflies? Do we stop to appreciate the beauty of nature? How long since a sunrise has bathed our face with the promise of a new day?

Getting out of touch with nature is a great loss. But the stars and seasons are patient and unpunishing, and they are always there for us. They will instantly welcome us home.

Today, let me renew my relationship with trees, birds, stars, and flowers.

Our life is like a jaunt in the mountains with unexpected views, turns in the way, resting places, and a goal we do not know.

> *Francois,*
> *Duc de la Rochefoucald*

We need the spirit of a pilgrim to begin a second career. First careers are born of time and necessity; second careers are born of the heart. Now it is finally our time to map out our life on our own course. Now might be the time to do something really different, to make an old dream come true. Can we throw our usual caution to the wind?

What kind of adventure will we find in the second half of our lives? Making a fantasy list is a great place to begin. A blank piece of paper and one hour of unin-terrupted time to really dream can open up whole new worlds, get us in touch with dreams we left behind. List everything and anything that comes to mind from living on a houseboat to joining the Peace Corps. Somewhere in our list we will discover the dream our intuition and spirit is guiding us towards. For each of us, the second part of life can be the best part.

Today, let me be an explorer in my own life.

February 21

Miracles are not extraordinary, they are
daily and ordinary.

Sarah T. Smith

A member of the American team that first climbed Mount Everest was returning from the peak and stopped to admire the view. Turning around he saw a small blue flower in the snow. At that moment, he said later, his life was changed. "Everything opened up and flowed together and made some strange kind of sense. And I was at complete peace."

How renewing are the moments when, for an instant, it all fits together. We humans need those beautiful jolts to recharge our hope. It is too easy to get caught up in the daily struggle. Necessary daily routines can dull us into a sleepwalking state.

But then, just before we get too complicated or forget the marvelous adventure we are on, the sky seems to open up and we get our own special miracles to restore our energy and wonder.

Today, let me watch for the miracles that are mine.

Nothing hurts worse than being ignored.
        Sam Friend

Cold, hard silences are often the most painful weapons one person can use against another. Nurturing a grudge can become a full-time preoccupation. Unspoken anger does not bring us freedom, but instead keeps us locked to the other person. The glue of unresolved resentment keeps us stuck in silent pain. Are there really people in our lives who have done things so bad that they deserve to be ignored?

Learning to assertively express our hurt and anger buys us emotional joy and freedom. We have found that our responsibility is to be honest, clear, and direct about our feelings and our needs. We need to learn when it's time to let go of old hurts and grudges.

When we develop the habit of clearing the air in relationships, we no longer feel helpless, no longer need to punish by ignoring and withdrawing into cold silence and we can then let our behavior be guided by joy, not pain.

Today, help me to forgive and let go.

February 23

In my life, I had touched all the bases . . .
a good career, a good marriage, good chil-
dren. I had had all the fun, met all the
responsibilities. But there was one little
piece missing.

Herman Gollob

When we have a piece of our life missing, the
icing on the cake never tastes just right. We might have
to dig deep to find our missing pieces, or sometimes
they wait just under the surface.

What are the things that continue to simmer on
our back burner? An adventure never taken? A ship
inside a bottle never finished? A play never written? A
walk along the Appalachian ridge?

Now is a good time to set some new life goals.
Putting these goals on paper will help bring them into
reality.

As we learn to look into our hearts, we begin to
recognize what is lacking in our lives. The answers are
there, just waiting for us to discover.

*Today, let me believe in my dreams and plan so they
can become reality.*

Of all my crimes, the breach of all the laws,
love soft, bewitching has been the cause.

Alphra Behn

Generations of hearts are universally connected by the power, agony, and joys of love. We all have love in common and for better or worse, it is the eternal link that connects us.

Faith in the healing power of love has been known to move great obstacles. When love calls, the answer is "Yes, I can! I will!" If there is any hope left in our tired hearts, healthy love will draw it out and help us trust yet again, one more time.

Love takes many forms and we grow to appreciate its shadings as we mature. We value the love of friends as well as family. We learn the value of tolerance and patience with those we love. And we learn to love ourselves, too, in a whole new way. In mid-life, we leave behind the shallow, demanding love of our youth, and find the deep glow of love that accepts without criticism.

Today, let me be open to give and receive love.

February 25

*He always imagined he would have a vigor-
ous old age. It hadn't been that way.*

James Sulter

Accepting that our healthy body can suddenly
betray us is one of the bitterest pills life asks us to swallow. We feel helplessly outraged when we are faced
with an illness that changes our lives. We are stunned,
and for a time everything seems to stand still. We are
unprepared to accept the betrayal of the healthy body
we took for granted for so many years. People we
know, only other people, get sick. We still had that
youthful idea that we were immune.

After the shock wears off, we find that we can
face illness in much the same way we faced every other
part of life. The internal resources we have come to
count on through the years will help us lay the founda-
tions of recovery. Courage helps us face the terror
ahead. Friends and family will help support us when
we feel our strength ebbing. A sense of humor brings
us a new perspective. And faith in the basic harmony
of life can help us find peace.

*Today, let me rediscover my inner resources and find
ways to use them with my illness.*

*There is no light without shadow and no
psychic wholeness without imperfection.*

> *C.G. Jung*

As we turn to face our shadow side, we can learn
to embrace our imperfections. Life's hard knocks
teach us to lighten up and be gentler with our character
defects. It's essential we develop compassion and a
sense of humor for ourselves and others. After all,
since we are human, we are bound to have defects. It's
in our nature. Why not learn to celebrate our defects
as well as our assets while we try to improve what
we can?

Slowing down allows us to realize that life is
about progress, not perfection. As we look around, we
begin to see that nothing is one-sided. Every thing,
every being, has a dark and a light side. The rain that
brings life to flowers also creates mud.

Making peace with our shadow side teaches us
about the gift of grace. Grace frees us to love ourselves for both our shadows and our light, and connects us with the shared humanity of one another.

*Today, let me remember that we are all imperfect
human beings worthy of love and compassion.*

February 27

*You may not be getting any younger but if
the best is yet to come, it will come only
if invited.*

Sam Levenson

In mid-life we are in a position to risk more than
we have ever had in the past. We have nothing to lose
and everything to gain if we decide to tackle anything
that intrigues us. When we cultivate a daily purpose,
we begin to experience life with zest. Alexandre
Dumas's Count of Monte Cristo had his daily purpose: He spent twenty years digging his way out of
prison with a teaspoon. When he succeeded, he cried
out, "The world is mine!"

Arthur Rubenstein, at the age of 80, was told he
was playing the piano better than ever. He replied,
"Now I take chances I never took before . . . . Now I
let go and enjoy myself, and to hell with everything
except music."

We can become risk-takers, too. We can live each
day to its fullest, enjoying everything that comes our
way. Every new day, we can wake and feel the world
is ours.

Today, let me dare to be all I can be.

We do not have to change for God to love us. He loves us exactly as we are at this moment.

Sam Friend

We can sometimes be very critical of ourselves as we review our lives. Parents, especially, may sometimes feel burdened with guilt, often when our children have problems. We feel responsible. The shortcomings of our past become our present-day monsters. "Why did I yell so much when he was little?" "I should have held her more." "Was I strict enough?" "Perhaps I should have been more interested in his school work." "She always said I was selfish, maybe it's true!"

We can actually wreck our present by reliving guilt from the past, by becoming so overwhelmed by yesterday's mistakes that we lock out today's joy.

We can learn from God's example. He loves us as we are, warts and all. He forgives our gravest errors. We can learn to treat ourselves with the same gentle kindness and acceptance. Today, we can focus on our successes, our talents, our many charms. In time, we can learn to love ourselves as He loves us.

Today, let me forgive myself for the past, knowing I did the best I could in that moment.

February 29

At the stroke of noon the descent begins.
And the descent means the reversal of all
the ideals and values that we cherished in
the morning.

C.G. Jung

The mornings of our lives have been spent as parents, nurturing our children. It is often difficult to push our young out of the nest, to let go. And it is hard for the young ones. Mother eagles have to remove the soft materials from the nest, leaving only sharp sticks too difficult to rest on.

It is a wrenching, painful process to liberate our children and reclaim our own lives. Many of us have spent so many years being defined as "Mom and Dad" that it's hard to know who we are now as individuals.

But in letting go we find a new identity and a new and glorious freedom. Now we can discover who we really are and what we really want. We can live our dreams and find a new life. With the scent of this new adventure in our nostrils, we can greet each day as a new opportunity for discovery, much as we did when we were small children.

Today, help me let go of my children and joyfully embrace my new life.

*The critical survey of himself and his fate
enables a man to recognize his peculiarities
. . . these insights are gained only through
the severest shocks.*

C.G. Jung

The realization that time is running out often
sparks an emotional crisis for us. A serious health
problem or the painful end of a relationship may cause
us to take a good look at our present lives. Carl Jung
writes that for those of us over thirty, all problems are
spiritual rather than psychological. More and more we
search for meaning in our lives. We struggle to make
sense of our world and try to fit ourselves into some
sort of correct destiny. Where are we going, and what
are our real bedrock values?

Time met halfway can prove to be our friend. We
can say, "Okay life, I'm committed to this ride, be my
teacher!" We can choose to open our minds to seeing
things in fresh new ways. We can choose to slow down
and be more fully aware of the present moment. After
all, this moment is all we have, all we've ever had. It is
all, really, that time consists of. And this moment is all
we need to continue to explore life.

Our search helps us learn who we are and what we
really want. We won't always like what we learn, but
if we keep an open mind, we will always enjoy the
education.

*Today, let me slow down enough for life to catch up
with me.*

March 2

*Sometimes a man hits upon a place to
which he mysteriously feels that he belongs
. . . Here at last he finds rest.*

W. Sommerset Maugham

We all long for that special spot that feels like
"coming home." It could be in the sun, the mountains,
or perhaps our own back yard. It will be a place for us to
really have good times, relax, and enjoy living.

Retirement is an art. It takes imagination, goal-
setting, and courage to arrange our lives as we really
want them to be. What if the place that calls to us is
two thousand miles away? Difficult decisions about
leaving family members and old roots will then need
to be made.

What if we need to go back to school or learn a
new skill? Some preparation and investigation will be
necessary before we start. What if we feel called to do
something our family or friends don't approve? Again,
we'll be faced with challenging choices between our
own wishes and those of others who care for us.

It isn't easy to let go of familiar ties and set out on
a mid-life adventure to parts unknown. Change is hard
at any age, but it is always possible if we believe we
have a right and privilege to enjoy life and do good
things for ourselves.

Today, help me listen to my heart.

*Forgiveness is always possible. Praying for
the willingness to forgive is the first step.*

Patrick O'Gorman

Do we know someone we can't forgive? What a
heavy burden, to carry pain and hurt from our past, to
stay tied to yesterday. Practicing the gentle art of forgiveness keeps us fully present in today and prepares a
serene foundation for tomorrow. When we are unwilling to forgive, negativity imprisons our energy and
power.

Letting go of past injuries may feel like a sacri-
fice. It is possible to nurse "justified anger" for so long
that it feels like a part of us. Will we look weak and
foolish if we give up our hate? Does forgiveness make
"them" right and us wrong?

Forgiveness is a risk in living and a positive affirmation of our own worth. Forgiveness is a gift we give
ourselves. It is the simple act of being bigger than any
problem. It is trusting that the loving part of ourselves
is stronger than the angry, vengeful part.

Forgiveness makes room for more love in our life.

*Today, let me trust that after the act of forgiveness I
will be given all the strength I need to move in new loving directions.*

March 4

If anything is worth doing, it is worth doing poorly.

Jim Quitno

Fear of failure can keep us paralyzed and not inactive, passive. We may become so afraid of not being perfect that we live in limbo. Unconsciously, we might feel protected by avoiding risks. If we don't try to reach a goal, we keep our illusions intact. We can always wonder if we would have made it, and dream about tomorrow when we might actually begin to take action. But we can lose all our todays in dreaming about the future.

Instead, we need to be willing to give up our illusions of perfection. We can learn to accept our humanity, and give ourselves permission to fail. We can give ourselves credit for small steps and less-than-perfect attempts. We can encourage ourselves to try again, or to try something different.

We no longer need to try to be perfect. Bit by bit, we can learn to take risks and become active right now, to accept our limitations, and to enjoy what success we have in spite of them.

Today, let me begin to follow one of my dreams by taking some action.

*I venture to say that at the bottom of most
fears, both mild and severe, will be found
an overactive mind and an underactive
body.*

Dr. Henry Link

Using our heads less and our arms and legs more
can often help quiet the savage beast we call fear. Fear
seems to grow fastest in an atmosphere of too much
thought and too little action. "Analysis paralysis" can
become a chronic condition.

To get out of our worry ruts, action is the magic
tonic. No matter how old we are, we can begin an
exercise program that will give us a positive uplift.
Research shows that exercise and physical activity are
natural mood and energy elevators, and help to
improve self-esteem.

For some of us, simply starting an exercise program may be harder than the actual exercise. But we
soon realize that using our bodies will bring more
slow, steady satisfaction than the quick fix of instant
gratification. An out-of-shape, underactive body asks
that we start off slowly.

The best way to begin a program is to stop thinking and just do it, letting go of our fears. For the first
thirty days, it will help if we stop analyzing. In time,
our bodies will take over, bringing up positive results.
Becoming reacquainted with our whole selves is a
gradual experience in self-love.

*Today, let me begin to exercise, even if it's walking for
ten minutes.*

March 6

How can you love the living world if you can no longer hear bird songs through the noise of traffic or smell the sweetness of fresh air?

James Lovelock

Our love affair with the planet is suffering from sensory deprivation. We are in danger of losing touch with the earth. Our giant cities help numb us to the changes in our environment—we become so accustomed to smoggy, hazy days that gray air begins to look natural to us.

What a loss it is to no longer see the stars at night or hear early morning bird calls. Our spiritual life suffers from the lack of clean air and the seasonal sounds and smells of Mother Earth. Country renewal trips are often necessary to put us back in touch with our senses.

Participation and support of environmental cleanup programs is a productive way for us to make a statement about the kind of world we want to live in, and the kind of world we want to leave as a legacy for our children.

Most of all, we can stay alert to the world around us, appreciating the wonders of nature. We can seek out healthy alternatives, and let our conscience—not our wallet—be our guide.

Today, let me plan to find some green grass to walk on and a starry sky to dream under.

The thing you desire is not only for you, but has already been started toward you out of the heart of God.

H. Emilie Cady

However we may define our Higher Power—as "God" or "Nature" or any other name, we can be certain that He gently infuses His good wishes for us into our hearts and minds. God plants the seeds of our healthy desires. Before we dream of a good and happy thing, He has wished it for us and is in the process of moving it into our lives. We have only to believe that we deserve our dreams to happen, then open ourselves up to receive happiness and abundance.

Many of us have a hard time believing happiness is our birthright. We may find it easy to accept that other people's lives are happy, but reject the idea that ours could be. We may feel that everything bad happens to us, and being happy is just not in the cards. We feel like lost sheep who are somehow different.

That kind of thinking can be dangerous. When we expect bad things to happen, we attract negative events and block our natural channels of health and happiness.

When we are willing to believe that God wants us to be happy and that we deserve to accept His gifts of joy and abundance, happiness and good events seem to find us. And goodness is there, if we open our hearts and minds.

Today, let me sweep the negatives from my thinking and open myself up to happiness.

March 8

*As healthy adults, we eventually come to
understand, as we play our friend, spouse,
parent, family roles, the limited nature of
every human relationship.*

                    Judith Viorst

Lucky people are loved unconditionally for the
first six months of their life. Many adult lives are desperately spent in unending expectations and searching
for that unconditional love. One task we have in our
own maturity is to recognize and accept our own limitations and the limitations of others. The seeds of
unhappiness are planted in the fantasy that we will be
loved perfectly one day, and will never again feel
lonely or insecure.

As we come to accept our own imperfections and
humanness, we realize that the people who love us the
most will sometimes hurt and disappoint us. We learn
to lighten up and forgive ourselves and others. We
even learn to love ourselves and others because of our
humanness, rather than in spite of it.

*Today, let me accept and learn to love the humanness
in myself, my family and friends.*

A good conscience is a continued Christmas.
Benjamin Franklin

A peaceful conscience allows us to fall asleep at night and not dread getting up in the morning. Nothing feels better deep down inside than knowing that we are committed to doing the right thing for ourselves and others.

Today, we don't have to be perfect. We don't always take the best or right action, but we are willing to learn, and willing to try to do things differently next time if necessary.

There are times in our life when we try to fool our conscience. Sometimes we want the easier, less painful solution to a problem. But only listening to our deep feelings and intuition seems to make our conscience happy. Learning to trust and respond to our internal reactions is the purest form of love we can practice, toward ourselves and others.

Today, I will follow my internal proddings, believing that they are my best teachers.

March 10

I'm only going to dread one day at a time.
Charles Schulz

Twenty-four hours is the gift life brings us each morning. We can tear it open and toss it aside, or slowly unwrap it and delight in its contents. No matter how we choose to open our daily gift, the quantity never changes. Each morning we have twenty-four hours to write into our personal history books.

Living in the daily now is an adventure in trust and risk-taking. We need courage to fully experience today, instead of regretting yesterday or living in tomorrow. To live fully in today asks that we trust it will be "enough," that we believe we are worthwhile and exactly where we should be at this moment in time. Living in today means being vulnerable and opening ourselves to our present reality.

The years are teaching us that one day at a time is all we can really handle and still keep our serenity.

Today, let me begin living in today.

*There is a difference between loneliness and
being alone; there is a choice of mind in
being alone, but loneliness comes up through
the heart into the throat.*

        William Faulkner

Loneliness eats up our insides. Its pain runs up
the very center of us. It even hurts physically to be
alone after the loss of a loved one. Every part of us
cries out in outrage and indignation. How dare this
happen? We want to fight back but have nothing to
fight against. The very worst of our pain seems to rise
up out of our feelings of helplessness.

We weren't ready to be alone. Who will really
love us now? Who else knows how we like our eggs?
What will we do when we wake up afraid and alone in
bed? So many little losses and memories all seem to
add up to an unbearable pain and feeling of being split
apart. Phrases like "Time heals" don't seem to help.

Perhaps there is little we can do except go through
the agony of loss. Living out and through the pain
might be the best gift we can give to the world today.
In time, we realize that time does heal all wounds. Our
pain lessens and we begin to look around again. We
find new people and places to be excited about. And,
finally, we discover we are no longer lonely.

*Today, let me acknowledge the depth of my loss. Help
me risk accepting a few small comforts from others.*

March 12

Self-pity is our worst enemy.
Helen Keller

Self-pity is often found crouched next to pain. When we feel stuck in a problem, self-pity and the resultant feelings of powerlessness are often the clues.

If we look closely, we may discover ourselves in a pattern of negative reactions and feelings of being unappreciated. Do we depend on others for approval, becoming stuck in discouragement and self-pity when we don't get the praise and attention we feel we deserve? Do we give too much, then feel angry and hurt when we don't get "enough" back?

When we constantly look for praise and appreciation from outside, we will never get enough. It's wonderful to be affirmed by others, but depending on the approval of family, friends, and co-workers to help us feel good can be an unhealthy substitute for self-love.

Today we are challenged to let go of self-pity no matter what our circumstances. We are challenged to claim and personally acknowledge our own gifts and resources. We no longer choose to wait for the permission and approval of others before we seize life.

Today, let me acknowledge that the validation of my personal worth is an "inside job."

*Your position [of authority] never gives you
the right to command. It only imposes on
you the duty of living your life that others
can receive your orders without being
humiliated.*

Dag Hammerskjold

An ability to blend power, compassion and kindness is the mark of a good leader. If we need to put others down in order to meet our goals, we will be second-rate leaders. To be compassionate in a position of power we must be personally secure and believe that we are good and adequate human beings. Effective leaders don't allow the needs of their own egos to dictate their decision-making. Immature leaders never seem to get enough power, prestige, praise, and money to feel secure. And this need to constantly be "on top" can kill the flower of compassion.

Where are the personal obstacles that stand in the way of our achieving excellence in our position of authority? Do we have some unmet ego needs that we could risk leaving behind? We can become better leaders by filling our own need for security. We may be struggling for perfection, instead of rewarding ourselves for our progress. By focusing on the issue rather than our own needs, we can develop objectivity. In time, we can become effective, compassionate leaders, respected by ourselves and others.

Today, help me put power to good use for everyone around me.

March 14

*How often will the vast emptiness astonish
me like a complete novelty and make me
say, "I never realized my loss until this
moment."*

C.S. Lewis

Some of life's losses feel like a kick in the stomach. Grief is as unpredictable as the March wind in its ability to blow back into our days when we least expect it. But losses do begin to heal through the spontaneous expression of feelings. Grief can't be planned. It seems to especially fill us in quick moments when our defenses are down. A great deal of healing happens in those moments because our deepest pain is expressed and purged. Little occurences and certain people and places may open up our emotional floodgates. A sight, sound or smell can bring all our feelings rushing back in an instant. But in time, peace replaces sorrow. Grief washes over and through us until its waves are spent, leaving peace and deep serenity in its place.

Today, let me believe that grief will take its own course and that eventually my ache will become bearable.

*Every day do at least one thing that will
bring you closer to your dreams.*

Silvester Rocco

Old photograph albums and pressed flowers in
sun-faded books are distant reminders of our parents'
and grandparents' lives. They were once so vibrant, so
full of their own living and loving.

Holding today in our hand may give us the illusion
that time could stretch on forever. In the midst of vigorous living, it's difficult to comprehend that we will
eventually be someone else's memory.

A social worker who spends her days with dying
patients shares the message she most frequently hears
at the side of deathbeds. The faces and voices are different but the words and urgency are the same: Live
life today to the fullest, listen to the wishes of your
heart. Don't put off your dreams until tomorrow.

Tomorrow we will be someone's memory—but
today belongs to us.

Today, help me seize the moment.

March 16

*Prince Charming had a flat tire somewhere
on the road to my life.*

Rachael McWilliams

Wanting and not having a good love relationship feels like a dull heartache that never really goes away. We may want a special relationship so much it is hard to understand why it evades us.

To be really known and loved by another human being is a fundamental need, and the older we get the more we appreciate the beauty and joy to be had in a loving relationship.

By defining our self throughout life, we now have a better sense of the real person we are. We know how much we have to share and give, and this knowledge may increase our heartache. We may long to share so many special moments, so much love. We may long for the double celebration of life and the awed feeling of gratitude that a special relationship or friendship brings.

At these moments, the only thing that seems to console us is to have absolute trust in our goodness and desirability, and trust in the goodness of our Higher Power. Believing that wonderful things are in God's plan for us helps us endure the times when we ache to be known, loved, and held by a dear one. Who knows what this new day will bring?

Today, let me trust that God's plan for me is exactly what I need.

Angels can fly because they take themselves lightly.

> *G.K. Chesterton*

Life takes on a new look when we learn to laugh at ourselves. Oversensitivity is a hard master and we find it difficult to relax when we're on guard and looking for criticism in other people's reactions and comments.

When we doubt our own value and work, we may be ready to strike out at any suggestion of criticism. Learning to relax and roll with the flow of life is a mark of our growing self-love and personal security.

The ability to laugh at our own shortcomings takes the tension out of our communications and relationships. We don't put ourselves down, but we learn to lighten up in tense moments.

And when we stop taking ourselves and the rest of the world so seriously, we begin to notice the positives in daily living and begin to expect good things to happen.

Today, let me grow in my ability to relax into life.

March 18

Eighty percent of life is showing up.
Ellen Goodman

Some days all we can do is put one foot in front of the other and keep going. The day-to-day living isn't always uplifting. There are days when it seems like an effort to make a morning cup of coffee. There seem to be periods in our life when no amount of positive thinking and cheerful self-talk can put a smile on our face and a bounce into our step.

These are gray days, down days, and "somewhere in the middle" days. Perhaps it's the beginning of the fall season, the days are getting shorter, and we feel blue. There may be a certain holiday letdown when we feel very much alone after celebrations and family times. Before and after vacations, during an illness, or suddenly in a quiet moment are some of the times that can plague us all with loneliness or depression.

But we make the effort, knowing good times are ahead if we are there to find them. The act of "suiting up and showing up" can be the best act of courage we can muster up in blue times. And sure enough, the bad times pass and the sun shines again, whether we are willing to believe it now or not, so why not believe?

Today, let me trust that the process of going through the routine of blue days as best I can is an accomplishment in living.

Desolation is the crippling experience of the shrinking circle of friends with the devastating awareness that the few years left to you to live will not allow you to widen the circle again.

Henri J. Nouwen

The loss of familiar ties sets us adrift. When friends who shared our history die or move away, we grieve the loss of these beloved connections. But we must look to the future with hope. Focusing on the past and staying stuck there empties the life from our hearts.

There was a man in his late seventies who had lived a vigorous and giving life. Still in robust health, a subtle change occurred in him the year before he died. He said that he was never lonely for his old friends who have recently died because they were still with him. In fact, he said he talked to them more and more. Intuitively and without resistance, he was making his transition. He was still very present and connected to those who loved him here as he began to embrace his own death and connect with old friends who died. But he never really lost anyone he loved.

Today, let me trust that the people I have loved will never really leave me.

March 20

*Spring fills my heart with so much awe that
I fear it might burst.*

Arleen Marie Smith

With each new spring, we shed another layer of
worldly distractions and get closer to our real insides.
Spring leaves us in constant amazement at all there is
to learn and experience in our flowering world. There
seem to be endless beautiful places to visit, books to
read, flowers to plant and water, redbirds to watch,
and lovely human beings to meet.

Sometimes we fear we do not deserve so much joy,
or we wait expectantly for it to end. But we are worthy
of happiness this great. We are reaping the benefits of
years of personal growth. We are learning to let go of
superficial distractions and concentrating on the awe
to be found in the moment.

Spring is an explosion of delight and well-being.
It is visible proof that we were made to enjoy and be
happy. It is a gift given again and again to hearts
already overflowing.

*Today, let me relish my feelings of gratitude and
wonder in the miracle of the daffodil and renewed
beginnings.*

Eighty years old: No eyes left, no ears, no teeth, no legs, no wind, and when all is said and done, how astonishingly well one does without them.

Paul Claudel

We have a choice to make as we age. Will we treat our advancing years as friend or enemy? Optimism, realism, and a sense of humor are good bedfellows in the process of aging.

We have little choice but to accept the physical impairments and changes. Chronic health problems are a fact of aging; we can accept them with grace or with resistance. But it is also possible to do quite well in spite of life's problems, aches, and pains. A sense of humor can get us through the toughest times, bringing fun and a healthy perspective to life.

Attitude, attitude, attitude—the one word that seems to distinguish those who live from those who just survive. We can change and reverse our attitude at any age if we are willing to learn to recognize and redirect our thoughts in a positive direction. It also helps if we can stick with winners and find happy, positive people to spend time with. It is never too late to begin planting our daily gardens with roses instead of poison ivy.

Today, let me find positive people to spend time with.

March 22

But true love is a durable fire
In the mind ever burning
Never sick, never old, never dead
From itself never turning.

Sir Walter Raleigh

Perfect romances are fantasies born of fairy tales and love songs. We may persist until the end of our days searching for the person who will make us happy. There is great joy in wanting to share our lives with a partner, but it's unhealthy to expect the other to be responsible for our happiness.

Love and intimacy flourish in relationships when there is a basic spiritual harmony between two people. The spark of our love relationships isn't physical but attitudinal. We are more and more drawn to people who embrace life without attack and judgment. We may love someone short, tall, round, or wrinkled if their soul clasps hands with ours.

Love is changing as we are changing. We no longer look for perfection, but are drawn to a feeling of shared humanness and celebration of life. Experiencing this with another is the exhilarating experience of happy love.

Today, let me be open to loving the joyous spirit in myself and others.

*Decide to be happy, knowing it's an atti-
tude, a habit gained from daily practice,
and not a result or payoff.*

Denis Waitley

Since we find it so central to our lives, it is sur-
prising that more of us don't target happiness as a primary goal to work toward. We can, in fact, actually
decide to be happy and then begin to actively seek that
goal.

On the road to happiness, our first task might be
to list on paper everything that stands in the way of our
being happy. We might want to discuss our list with
someone we trust in case it contains items that would
sabotage us or subconsciously keep us stuck. Having
made a decision to be happy, and armed with our list,
the next step is to work through the obstacles one by
one and to praise ourselves for each step we take, however small.

Blocks to happiness include habitual negative
thoughts. Becoming aware of this self-talk and gradually substituting the old tapes with new will slowly
change our attitude about happiness. We'll begin to
believe we deserve it. Out of this belief, this movement
towards happiness, we may be surprised to find that
we're happy along the way.

Today, let me be as happy as I make up my mind to be.

*When we are in doubt as to whether we
have offended God, we must humble ourselves, request God to excuse us, and ask
for more enlightenment for another time,
and forget what has happened and return to
our accustomed way.*

St. Francis de Sales

We exercise humility by accepting reality, accepting what is. When we find it hard to be humble perhaps it's because we're not willing or able to see
ourselves as worthy of forgiveness. If we refuse to
believe we've done something that requires forgiveness, we can't say we're sorry. We remain attached to
the situation and can't get on with our lives.

Conversely, to see our actions as unforgivable is to
veer into grandiosity and egocentricity. Believing that
God will not forgive us is like making decisions for
God. Humility means accepting our humanness, our
limitations, our worth, and God's forgiveness.

How freeing it is to wake up each morning with
the knowledge that we begin each day with a clean
slate, trusting that God loves us so much that we may
begin again the instant we are willing. To God, we are
as infinitely lovable today as we were at the moment of
our birth.

Today, let me be humble enough to accept my goodness.

But I do not have all the answers, either.
Especially when things go very wrong, and
we are thrown into tragedy—at times like
these I feel very much in the dark.

Mariam Makeba

Those of us who have experienced natural disasters
or traumas—fires, hurricanes, accidents, floods, theft
—have learned something of life's priorities. Perhaps
we've curled up into a ball of self-pity, outraged at the
disruption to our lives. After a while, however, even
when we've lost our most valued and irreplaceable possessions, we feel foolish. Life alone is essential.

Disasters are great equalizers. In spite of ourselves, true humility creeps in, the gratitude for simply being alive. In the most fundamental of ways we
experience our link with other human beings and can
maintain this link, and our sense of gratitude, by helping those less fortunate. Our new wisdom as a survivor
begins. And with the strength we gain as we go
through these trials, we come to know that we will
survive more. So our fear begins to vanish, and we are
freer to fully live.

Today, let me rediscover my common bond with all
humanity.

March 26

*It appears . . . that some development of
the capacity to be alone is necessary if the
brain is to function at its best and if the
individual is to fulfill his highest potential.*

Anthony Storr

As we approach the end of our prime years, the
need for time alone can be a true hunger and thirst,
and this points to an authentic spiritual need. Fishing,
quiet long walks, or just plain sitting in solitude can be
as important to our well-being as maintaining satisfying relationships.

Too much of the time we are plunged into the
noisy busyness of everyday life that conspires to keep
us in a state of activity and togetherness with other
people.

We need to make a commitment to some selfish
space and time, where there is no one to impinge on
our consciousness. When we need to, we can return to
this place and state of mind frequently.

In our moments of solitude, we find ourselves
becoming connected; creativity can emerge, and we
feel whole. Self-discovery and self-realization are the
fruits of solitude. When we can enjoy being alone, we
can be sure we are growing mature.

*Today, let me take time for solitude to be in touch with
the depths of my being.*

*The rewards from detachment are great:
serenity—a deep sense of peace; the ability
to give and receive love in self-enhancing,
energizing ways; and the freedom to find
real solutions to our problems.*

Melody Beattie

Some of us have spent years, if not decades, trying to change other people, places, and things only to
find to our dismay that we have failed. Tired and bone
weary we may finally get the message that we aren't in
charge of others. True, we may truly know "a better
way" for them but we find that they insist on doing
things their way in spite of our best efforts, manipula-
tion, bargaining, pleading, and threats.

Sooner or later, we must surrender and let go of
our involvement in the problem. When we lovingly
detach from the problem but not the person we begin
to understand the difference between living in our
solution or living in their problem.

Life doesn't operate on our timetable and we are
beginning to understand that we can still have peace
even while living in difficult situations. Learning to
focus healing energy in our own lives is the beginning
of freedom for ourselves and others.

*Today, let me learn to lovingly detach from trying
to control other people and help me live well in my
own life.*

March 28

It's a steady job.

Samuel Rosenthal

Samuel Rosenthal worked for the H.A. Eisner Window Shade Company in Manhattan for over eighty-four years. The word retirement didn't fit into Samuel's vocabulary.

In the best of all worlds, we would decide when we would like to retire. Each of us carries a different biological clock that lets us know the best age for us to stop active employment. Many of us are reaching our peaks at age sixty-five when we are abruptly put out to pasture.

Mid-life is the time to start thinking and planning for the next half of our lives. Creative planning will help us avoid retirement shock and its resultant depression. We need to believe we can continue to be the masters of our own fate as we grow older. Planning and goal setting are important mid-life activities that are based on an open inventory of our likes and dislikes. Are we ready to retire? If not, how can we prepare to remain active in a profession after the mandatory retirement age. Active involvement in mid-life career planning is a gift we deserve to give ourselves.

Today, let me step off the sidelines of my life and walk into the main arena of actively planning for myself.

*Nearly every morning as he woke up, he
would turn and look into my eyes and say,
"How could I possibly be so lucky?"*
  Diane Kennedy Pike

When a marriage or relationship is developed and
healthy, it takes on a life of its own. Awe, graciousness,
and respect shine from such a union and it rubs off on all
of us. There is no way to contain and isolate this kind of
loving energy; it fills rooms and gives hope to those of us
who struggle with more hurting relationships.

How these couples develop and nurture such a
bond is no secret. Most of them talk out their problems
instead of burying them, and they behave kindly
toward one another so it feels safe to talk. They may
meet at least once a week to let go of unfinished emotional business. They both probably have a sense of
humor, have separate as well as mutual interests, and
each day practice forgiveness and gratitude.

These attitudes, these ways of being, come naturally to few of us, especially those of us in healthy relationships. We've had to work consciously to coax them
forth, and then work to maintain them. But one way
we can begin to build such a union—whether we're in
one or not—is by being grateful for kindness and love
wherever we find it.

*Today, let me believe that it is possible to have a beau-
tiful, loving relationship.*

March 30

Appropriate guilt is a good motivation for change. Chronic guilt is a way to punish self and others.

Maria Spencer

There is a story about a psychologist who had amazing success in helping chronic pain sufferers. The simple advice he gave them was, "Each time you pass a mirror, glance at yourself and holler, 'Not Guilty.'"

Guilt is literally a "pain in the neck," or back, or stomach. Guilt can tear up our insides up and drain our energy. Guilt-ridden people develop a habit of continuously reliving their lives and find themselves wrong. Years of holding on to guilt shrinks our self-esteem and erodes our confidence, often to the point of causing real physical and emotional illness.

Self-honesty and sharing are the tools we need to begin our recovery from a chronic guilt and self-blame cycle. Getting honest about this with another human being is a good place to begin. Usually we find that we punish ourselves too harshly. Breaking the guilt habit will take our concentrated effort, but in the long run it will take less energy than licking the stamps to mail out payments for doctor bills.

Today, let me learn to forgive myself.

*Like my own father, I want my son to be
normal. I am prepared to ruin his youth
if that's what it takes.*

Stanley Bing

Our children are not us. They are separate, distinct persons who usually don't try to please us. Sometimes we try to break them as a cowboy would break a horse for a rodeo. Sadly we find that, after a certain age, they are unbreakable. We only get saddle sores from trying. Our children have minds of their own and not only won't practice our best advice, they don't even want to hear it.

We will never win power struggles with our children. If we have a need to be "right" as our children grow up, we will never allow ourselves to enjoy their growth.

Learning how to help a young person save face is the exercise of a wonderful wisdom and is a precious gift to our children. Some days our best hope is the belief that most difficult times are developmental phases that will pass whether or not we have patience. Knowing this, we can do our loving best, then sit back and enjoy our family's growth.

Today, let me learn that give-and-take is necessary to live with my growing children.

April 1

*Total me and total you and total us together,
and the sum is the same, only the center is
different.*

George F. Simons

We will always be alone in our heart of hearts.
This part of us was meant to experience and explore
solitude. Our spiritual centers belong only to us, and
were never meant to be healed, fixed, or made full by
lovers, parents, or friends. Perhaps they are our pipe-
lines to God.

Many of us struggle against our center. We feel a
hollowness that we sometimes flee in panic. We passionately seek out others to "complete" us and fill the
void in our hearts, but we find that our search is desperate because the aloneness never really goes away.
We may temporarily quiet it in the arms of a lover but it
soon returns.

Perhaps we are meant to embrace our aloneness
instead of running from it. Perhaps we will finally
find peace when we have the courage to use our own
resources to fill this need.

*Today, let me have the courage to stop running from
myself.*

*We must never hesitate to ask God for the
most difficult things. The more difficult
things are to grant, the more we must ask
for them, believing that God loves us
passionately.*

Charles de Foucauld

It is a leap of faith to believe that God loves us
abundantly and to believe, further, that God is leading
us to our heart's desire. There is no contradiction in
praying for what we really want and also affirming,
"Thy will be done." These two attitudes may look like
polar opposites, but at some point beyond our field of
vision they converge. We just can't see it yet.

That's where faith comes in. We dream, desire,
and imagine for good reason. We yearn for something
better because God would have us be better, growing
as all creation grows, continually giving birth to
ourselves.

Would God expect us not to ask for our heart's
desire? That it is our heart's desire is proof enough of
God's perfect will. When we ask, we receive, and we
often receive more than we can imagine.

*Today, let me believe that God grants me difficult
challenges to prove to me the vastness of His love.*

April 3

My father drank. He drank as a gut-punched boxer gasps for breath, as a starving dog gobbles food—compulsively, secretly, in pain and trembling.

Scott Russel Sanders

Children of alcoholics or other kinds of sick families are not scarred for life. They are instead wounded survivors with many gifts. Those of us who are in recovery have spent years blaming ourselves for every trouble that strikes our children. If we are recovering alcoholics, for instance, perhaps now is the time to forgive ourselves for having a disease we were not responsible for. We were not responsible, but we are accountable.

Being accountable means making amends. It means taking whatever steps our recovery requires and choosing to live in health other than disease. It doesn't mean taking responsibility for our children's problems —to do so is to rob them of the opportunity to work through their difficulties and grieve their losses. It means having the courage to forgive ourselves and get on with our lives.

Perhaps we need to focus on what we did right and to look at our children as gifted and resourceful rather than damaged. If we believe this about them they'll come to believe it about themselves, and in turn to believe they deserve what in the past we may not have been able to give.

Today, let me focus on the health in myself and in my children. This healthy attitude will instantly begin to lift some of my pain and guilt.

*The search for my own God was a deeply
personal journey into myself and beyond
and I wouldn't trade the God I found for
another version.*

Jeanette Hope

Discovering a Higher Power that makes sense to
us is a serious business that may take us most of the
years of our lives. Some of us grew up with a relationship with God that has been marked by its stability, a
relationship that has stayed in place throughout the
years. For many of us, however, struggling, redefin-
ing, exploring, and questioning have characterized our
spiritual search.

Each personal spiritual journey appears to be
exactly that: personal. To look into the needs and character of others, to prescribe for them a living formula
to match ours, is a risky business that often pushes us
farther away from our own path.

We each have an inalienable fight to define the
Higher Power we would seek and to define what it
means to be spiritual. Once we claim this right, and
with it the right to uncertainty and struggle, we tap
into a wisdom born of our own lives, a wisdom that
may suggest that it is not only we who are looking for
God, but God who is looking for us.

*Today, let me focus on my own spiritual journey, confi-
dent that I will know what to say to others.*

April 5

*Don't focus on how you want to look, but
how you want to feel about your looks.*

Rita Freedman

Our self-esteem mirrors the way we feel about our
bodies. As we grow older, it is healing to befriend our
bodies and to practice loving them exactly as they are.
The paradox of change is that it begins with acceptance. By accepting our bodies today, as they are, we
will be less likely to distrust and sabotage the positive
changes to come.

To practice accepting our bodies today, first we
have to really look at ourselves. Then we need to touch
and massage. Years of judging ourselves, of seeing our
bodies as ugly and inferior, has caused many of us to
emotionally disown our physical selves. It takes work
to get ourselves back, and at first we have to do a lot of
pretending, but gradually we see the judgments—and
hear the voice who says them, whether it's ours or
another's—for what they are: like any judgment, they
originated in fear, fear of the other, of anything different, and we no longer need to beat ourselves with a
club we never chose.

*Today, let me love and accept my body exactly as it is.
Help me practice this acceptance until I begin to feel it.*

*She was not the first wife to sit by a dying
husband's bedside imprisoned by his illness.
She was not the first to come to pity herself
as much as the patient.*

I.S. Coooper

Living with the illness of a loved one can drain us
physically, emotionally, and spiritually. It can "pull the
plug" of our energy, dragging us down into the pits of
depression and exhaustion. It may be difficult for us to
understand that we can love someone and at the same
time feel angry with him or her. We may even get mad
at someone who has a disease he or she didn't cause.
Feelings aren't facts; they are just our feelings.

It is natural to have a range of reactions toward
our loved one's illness. We may feel depressed, panicky, and guilty. We may be filled with rage. If we
spend enough time around a sick person, we may also
despair of our inability to make him or her well, and
slide into self-pity.

To find grace and serenity during this time, we
need to be gentle with ourselves and accept all our
feelings as valid. We need time out, we need support,
and we need safe people to talk to—people who will let
us have all our feelings. Only by caring for ourselves
can we be any good to someone else.

Today, let me nurse myself as well as my sick partner.

April 7

*This we know. The earth does not belong to
man; man belongs to the earth. Man did not
weave the web of life; he is merely a strand
in it. Whatever he does to the web, he does
to himself.*

Chief Seattle

When we realize that all the earth's peoples are
linked first by the laws of nature and distantly second
by human-made political and economic institutions,
national and political borders dissolve.

Environmental pollution respects no political
boundary. It affects us all. We can no longer deny that
our health is dependent on the health of the environment. We must face the facts of dwindling resources,
species extinction, and environmental degradation.

Responsible solutions are expensive, but we continue to ignore long-term effects over short-term
profits only at our peril. In our growth, we've learned
how not to inflict violence on ourselves. Let us do the
same for Mother Earth.

*Today, let me pledge my attention to environmental
concerns as a citizen of the world.*

*Being engaged literally means being excited
in any sense of the word about any task . . .
looking forward to whatever it is you're
doing.*

Tom Peters

Striving to reach our fullest potential and to use
our talents in any sphere can be labeled a career. Most
of us have shifted directions and modified our careers
several times during our prime working years. Are we
satisfied where we are now?

If we are still writing off most of our waking
hours; if we yearn to work with more dedication, zest,
intensity, and even joy, we may need to examine where
we're using our best energies. Now is the time to pause
and consider changing our careers.

There are more avenues open to us now than there
used to be—more and better ways to use the best that is
in us. And now we can appreciate and honor skills and
aptitudes we used to dismiss.

As we grow older and wiser, we attract increasingly better things—including careers—into our lives.
We need only choose a direction and step out.

*Today, let me be grateful for my many talents, even
those I have not yet discovered.*

April 9

*If I had to do it all over again, I'd learn to
tell them to go to hell.*

Frank Mankiewicz

We have arrived at the glorious period in our lives
when we realize some people don't really like us,
loathe us, in fact. A few of our colleagues, a couple of
family members, perhaps. We see this as a tribute,
finally, to our integrity. At last, we are defining ourselves more clearly!

In earlier years we were so damned agreeable; we
blended in, we were bland, and we had an intense need
to be liked. Approval from our fellows was the chief
barometer of how we felt about our ourselves. This
need for approval governed our decisions and made us
dishonest at times. Our identity is more solid now, and
we are comfortable with it. We make clear statements,
take stands on issues, have opinions, and see nothing
unpleasant in sticking to them. We can be downright
outspoken at times.

Are we narrow-minded? Not at all. We still listen
and reflect and acknowledge the right of others'
views. Nevertheless, we've given up placating people
and acting so flexible we felt nameless. Now we are
willing to stand up and be seen for who we are, and to
be proud to do so.

Today, let me say and act who I am.

*What a lovely surprise to finally discover
how unlonely being alone can be.*
                    Ellen Burstyn

Mid-life finds many of us thrust into living alone for the first time. How frightening it seems—the unnatural quiet, being at loose ends with too many thoughts and with no one to talk to.

Although we may sorely miss the presence of another person, this can become a time of discovery. We had assumed loneliness would overtake us, yet we may well find the opposite to be true. In our solitude we can discover the joy of our own creativity in a new hobby—perhaps we might even renew an old pastime from our youth.

The dangers of isolation, sheer selfishness, and withdrawal are real when we are alone. Yet once we recognize these dangers we can make appropriate room and time for socializing. Solitude is a time for action, even if that action is as quiet as meditation. When we find the activities that give us joy, we can easily allow ourselves to be alone and end up liking it just fine!

Today, let me refuse to equate aloneness with loneliness.

April 11

*Keeping our eyes on the prize means not
getting sidetracked by trivia.*

Gerard Vanderhaar

In mid-life we begin the process of examining
ourselves and redirecting our energies. We realize we
want more time for reflection—long walks or being
quietly alone for reassessing and renewing ourselves.

We come to value the twenty-four hours each day
offers and learn to bypass trivia and time-wasters
which drain our resources.

We may go through times when we often shift
gears and alter the course we've been taking. We want
to look for values that will endure, activities that enrich
us, and increasingly we turn away from superficial
matters. These are all choices we make which are
based on the wisdom of experience. Even when we
feel confused or depressed because we've spent years
headed in a direction that no longer suits us, we are
growing wiser. It's our experience that brings us this
awareness. Confusion may only be an openness to
change that we've never allowed ourselves before, and
we are never too old to change.

*Today, let me sense what is truly worthy and precious
to me in my mid-life.*

*"What'll we do with ourselves this after-
noon?" cried Daisy, "and the day
after that, and the next thirty years?"*
    F. Scott Fitzgerald

When we're recuperating from a long illness or
beginning retirement we may have intense feelings of
uselessness or boredom. Most work situations have
provided us with the freedom from having to make
tough choices about our use of time. What do we tell
ourselves when we no longer have regular work to take
up our days?

We can expect that we will sometimes be bored.
The natural ebb and flow of life is cyclical. Sometimes
we feel too busy, and other times we're bored.

We will be offered advice by well-meaning
friends and relatives, but they are not walking in our
shoes. We are responsible for being bored as well as
for dealing with it. The solution is not a lot of mean-
ingless activity, but meaningful activity tailor-made to
our needs. Boredom is a message. It tells us we now
have the opportunity to try new things, to make new
choices about our time and our activities.

*Today, let me realize boredom lasts forever only if do
nothing about it.*

April 13

*I am alone here in New York, no longer a
we.*

Elizabeth Hardwick

The heavy sadness experienced through death or
divorce or moving far away is certainly for ourselves
and for the one now absent, but also we mourn the loss
of our dreams.

The dream was our illusion of how things should
have been. We had counted on our lives running
smoothly like a predictable old-fashioned novel. But
the rest of our lives won't be exactly what we once
expected or hoped for. We must unload those dreams if
we want the rest of our lives to be healthy. Our dreams
were once a treasure, now we grieve the loss and let
it go.

Slowly starting over again is the challenge. We
tiptoe, frightened and confused, as into icy water. We
learn to value friendships more, and somehow learn to
live without the old dreams, without our special person. Soon, when we're ready in the space left by our
loss will come a new dream, a new special person better suited to our lives as they are today.

*Today, let me realize that the only totally dependable
person I have is myself.*

*Try a thing you haven't tried before three
times, once to get over the fear, once to find
out how to do it, and a third time to find
out whether you like it or not.*

> *Virgil Thomas*

Overcoming a fear calls for acceptance, forgiveness, and action. First, we truly accept and forgive ourselves for being afraid. If facing our fear is in our best interest, then we act. We may still be afraid but we do it anyway.

If we wait to understand perfectly and be totally free of our fears, we might never act. Facing our dreads takes away their power to harm us and connects us with our resources.

We can jump into life at any age. Becoming a risk-taker begins with a decision to reach out and experience more of living. Some of us who have stood on the sidelines and played it safe are deciding to take a leap of faith and get into the heart of things.

We each have a one-way ticket to be used as we wish. We can choose to view the scenery from the security of our compartments, or we can throw open the doors and leap out into life.

Today, let me take one risk and begin planning to do one thing I have dreamed about.

April 15

Do what you can, with what you have, with where you are.

Theodore Roosevelt

When we bloom where we are planted, we grow healthy roots grounded in reality. Making the best of life is what all happy people seem to be about. Taking action is our best guarantee of physical and emotional health.

When we look around us we can choose to see roses or thorns. We have painfully come to know that we can't change other people, places, or things, but we can change ourselves and our attitudes. We can choose to accept reality as it is today and make the best of it. True, we may change it again tomorrow, but today we are living in the present and we have a choice to make. We can choose to be angry and resentful that life isn't easier, or we can build an attitude of gratitude and live fully in the reality of the day we've been given. Which kind of life do we want? It's our choice, and the only time we're given to make it is the present.

Today, let me believe that no one has the power to ruin my day.

*The degree to which I can create relation-
ships which facilitate the growth of others as
separate persons is a measure of the growth
I have achieved in myself.*

　　　　Carl R. Rogers

People in healthy, loving relationships give each
other the "gift of wings" to make their individual
dreams come true. When love is wise, it realizes that
each partner has special gifts to develop and contribute
to living, the development of which makes them more
of who they really are.

We seem most truly alive when the ones we love
give us their encouragement and blessings to develop
our potential. Wise loving gives each of us room to
breathe and grow.

Some of us fear that a spirit of freedom will cause
those we love to leave us and in our fear of abandon-
ment, we hang on tight and work to put walls around
our love. In a healthy relationship the "gift of wings"
allows us each to soar, then gratefully return with an
abundance of love and gratitude to celebrate and share
with our partner.

*Today, let me get honest in my appraisal of my rela-
tionships. Do I build bars and locks or encourage
wings in the people I love?*

April 17

We will have to give up the hope that if we try hard, we somehow will always do right by our children. . . . We will sometimes do wrong.

Judith Viorst

There is no such thing as a perfectly wise parent. We all goof up at times. No matter how well-intentioned we are, we will make mistakes with our children. We may "over-advise" them. We may be too smothering with our affections, or not affectionate enough. We may push them so hard to achieve that they fail in order to assert their independence. We may not give enough encouragement and then feel at fault when they flounder around indecisively.

Sooner or later we will need to make peace with our strengths and weaknesses as parents and forgive ourselves for being human. None of us bring a full array of talents to the task of parenting. The older we get, the more we learn about what we "should" have done differently. Perhaps the best lesson we are learning is that "should" is a useless word. We did the best we could and we are still doing our best. This is all life can ask of us.

Today, let me focus on the strengths and assets in both my children and myself and learn to let go of my "shoulds."

*The deeper that sorrow carves into your
being, the more joy you can contain.*

Kahlil Gibran

By suffering pain and loss, we have become
weathered and tough in our broken places. In the heart
of our suffering we come face to face with our own
helplessness and mortality. This journey into powerlessness and sorrow seems to put notches on our souls.
We are faced with puzzles without apparent solution.

The best that may come from our journey of sorrow is knowing we did survive, broken but also
healed, the bearers of a deeper compassion for the
human condition.

We grow wise through our pain and gain a more
balanced perspective. We are more able to offer help
and sympathy to others while not interfering with their
pain. This strength also enables us to cultivate joy in
our lives, even in the soil of grief.

Today, let me see through my pain to my strength.

April 19

Set your sights high, the higher the better. Expect the most wonderful things to happen, not in the future but right now.

Eileen Caddy

Miracles are not extraordinary. They are commonplace events that happen at the perfect moment. Small daily miracles are like flowers that bloom for us to pick and cherish. We can develop a talent for recognizing miracles and be introduced to wondrous gifts.

Even something as small as looking up into a winter sky and seeing the stream of a falling star not only leaves us awed by a moment in time, it is a miracle and we are part of it. Unexpectedly meeting a dear old friend on a day when nothing went right feels like sunshine after a storm. Other miracles might be opening the mail box and getting a check on the day when we needed it the most, or feeling stuck in a problem and suddenly recognizing the solution, or getting a hug from a child when we've gotten too serious.

These are reminders that we are part of a larger plan, and if we keep alert and expect miracles, we'll see them happen right before our eyes.

Today, let me see the world through my positive glasses.

*Middle life is definitely a time to have a
healthy respect for eccentricity. This is only
possible when we overcome the habit of
trying to please everyone.*

> *Gail Sheehy*

To follow the dictates of our inner spirit, we will
need to strike out in new and bold directions. When
we become more ourselves we find we need to learn to
say no to people and situations we used to say yes to.
We find we are not indispensable to anyone and, to our
dismay, we find many of the people we used to care-
take seem to do a great job of running their own lives
all by themselves.

Now that we have the freedom to really do our
own thing and please ourselves, we are in a position to
take risks and begin long overdue personal adventures.
Perhaps we will wear pink carnations in our hair and
orange and green socks as we begin to learn what truly
pleases us, whether it be perfectly traditional or outra-
geously eccentric. Or, more seriously, we may decide
to move to another climate a thousand miles away, or to
take up rock climbing or skydiving. In living our own
lives and no one else's, we are living to the fullest.

*Today, let me look in the mirror and greet the day as
my own person.*

April 21

Memory is history recorded in our brain, memory is a painter, it paints pictures of the past and of the day.

Grandma Moses

As we get further away in time from traumatic, painful events, it is easier to revise our version of what really happened. For years we may only have been able to feel our agony, and we needed to forget. We tried hard to cut out that awful part of our past in order to lead our lives with some degree of sanity.

Now we are granted a new insight: perhaps we overhear a phrase, another's conversation about a similar event, and the door opens for us to reexamine what happened so long ago.

When we look at painful memories, we can often see an opportunity for growth hidden there. Perhaps we've become stronger in spite of the pain, knowing we can survive. Or we've grown more careful, more responsible. Perhaps our lives have been pointed in a new, undreamt-of direction, and things have worked out for the best. This helps us begin to soften the hardness we've lived with for so long.

Today, let me realize my true peace of mind will come when the pieces of my past are healed.

*One of the most debilitating factors in con-
temporary society is forced retirement at
what is frequently the still-productive age of
sixty-five.*

Dr. Paul Yonggi Cho

At the age when we have learned most about life
and living, we are asked to retire from our careers.
George Burns says that "retirement at sixty-five is
ridiculous. When I was sixty-five, I still had pimples."
At age sixty-five we can expect to live many more productive years. We are at our best emotionally, spiritually, and often physically.

Sommerset Maugham wrote brillantly until age
ninety-two. Carl Sandburg and Robert Frost created
poetry well into their eighties. Marc Chagall painted
into his nineties. Grandma Moses began her art career
at seventy-two. Gustav Eckstein began learning Rus-
sian at age eighty-five to facilitate his work in Pavlov.
Marian Hart flew the Atlantic alone at age eighty-
three. Georgia O'Keeffe painted the southwest landscape vigorously into her nineties. On his ninety-ninth
birthday Thomas Bridson climbed a 2,000-foot mountain. Mid-life can be compared to a banquet in which
all our knowledge, dreams, and gifts are spread out
before us, and it is up to us to choose what we want to
enjoy for the continuing feast that is life.

*Today, let me come to know that I can be old at forty
or young at eighty.*

April 23

*One of the most urgent duties we owe to
God is to be afraid of nothing.*

Charles de Foucauld

Charles de Foucauld was a French hermit who
prayed in a thatch hut in the African desert. He did his
writing on a packing case that served as a table. To
save precious lamp oil, he wrote his meditations by the
light of the desert stars. His life was spent in an
unceasing search after the will of God. He followed
his call with passion and zest, putting his fears aside to
listen to his spirit and intuition.

We are all explorers in our own lives. We have also
been called for a special task. No one else ever born is
exactly like us or can contribute to life what we have
been challenged to share. When we trust that our journey is guided, we are better able to gently lay our fears
aside and listen to our spiritual voice. The more we
respond to our intuition the more "right" and directed
life becomes. Making friends with our intuition is
always an experience grounded in joy.

*Today, let me listen to the small, still voice of my spiri-
tual intuition that guides me in my play and work and
teaches me about my joyous gifts.*

The year's at the spring,
The day's at the morn; . . .
God's in his heaven,
All's right with the world!

Robert Browning

No feeling has ever been quite like the throbbing excitement of spring fever. It comes to us on a fine blue day, a day so clear that a bittersweet longing is pulled up from our deepest parts. The air smelling and tasting of pure life and popping buds just seems to take us out of time, out of our mundane lives for a while.

Windows open and white curtains blow as we air out winter's old smells. Some days there is too much loveliness to see, smell, and feel. Every new year we live seems to deepen our amazement at so much beauty given again so freely.

Spring is the time to get our hands and hearts into the turned earth. It is feeling the sun on our backs and working out the kinks of time and strain. And it is more, it is holding life inside ourselves as we embrace new life, old loves, and our own hearts.

Today, let me open up the windows of my heart to greet spring as a beautiful child coming home once again.

April 25

*We should always keep our eyes fixed on the
immense love God has for us . . . which
makes it so sweet, pleasant and natural to
Him to give us the greatest blessings.*

Charles de Foucauld

We can develop a "prosperity consciousness" and
expect our financial needs to be abundantly met. Worrisome obsessions about money rob us of joy and
energy. We might become so concerned about our
financial troubles that we lose the ability to relax and
enjoy living. But with the attitude that our Higher
Power will always be there to give us our "daily
bread" if only we ask for it, we need never feel
deprived or desperate.

Daily prosperity affirmations and visualizations
can quickly plant the seeds of abundance in our consciousness. It can be as simple as saying, "Give me
this day my daily bread." As we practice affirming
our financial and emotional health, we are automatically blessed with ideas and inspirations about ways to
find financial peace of mind. God will provide everything we need, even if it isn't always just exactly what
we want at the time.

*Today, let me know I am blessed with financial
abundance.*

> *Marriage can be a dumping ground and*
> *scapegoat for personal mid-life*
> *dissatisfaction.*
>
> *Jerome McFall*

Mid-life may bring a sense of urgency that can wreak havoc on a marriage. A panicky "do or die" feeling may erupt in what is termed a mid-life crisis.

Our individual redefinition is a task that often involves role reversals for men and women. We women find ourselves becoming more assertive and independent as we men become more responsive to our emotions. Redefinition and change is a balancing act that challenges couples in new and compelling ways. Those of us who manage to ride out the storms of each other's changes and passages are in a unique position to negotiate and renew our commitments. When the dust settles, it is possible to view marriage from a more honest vantage point.

Who are we now? What are our values and goals? How are we willing to negotiate and adjust to make our new pieces fit? When we engage in the process of finding these answers together, we are already enjoying the rewards of our new maturity.

Today, let me ride out the storm of my unrest and make no decisions about my marriage until I feel more grounded in myself.

April 27

*Never lose an opportunity of seeing any-
thing that is beautiful; for beauty is God's
handwriting—a wayside sacrament.*

Ralph Waldo Emerson

When we feel particularly drab and dreary, let us
consider adding an experience of beauty and pleasure
to our day. This is an action we can take any time,
though we rarely approach it so directly.

When we yearn for something lovely, we want
a richness to enhance our perspective and ennoble
us beyond our routine. We can easily find color,
texture, shapes, or sounds that delight us and fire our
imagination.

Reading poetry out loud, seeing a sentimental
children's movie, listening to an old record or playing a
Bach Cantata, feeling running water flow and splash-
ing it awhile, visiting a bakery as today's bread is
brought out—any of these can lift us above the hum-
drum. When we consciously take time and make the
effort to give this to ourselves, we are giving ourselves
the gift of an active, thoughtful, self-loving life. We
are also practicing gratitude for the boundless opportunities which surround us all the time.

*Today, let me seek out something beautiful so I may see
and hear with freshness, and be refreshed.*

*Love always means going to others not
demanding that they come to you.*

    Paul Tournier

Demanding people are difficult to be around.
They seem to charge the air with tension when they
enter a room. Demanding people don't seem to give
others a chance to move toward them. They are too
busy complaining because they aren't getting what
they want.

Does this sound familiar? Does it sound like us
sometimes? It has been said that those who learn how
to live peacefully with a demanding person will have
earned a place in heaven. Do we want to earn a place
in heaven this way? Do we want to be this way? Probably not. But sometimes we don't feel we are good
enough to be loved, so we demand and grab for love
and attention. Usually we end up with empty hands
and a stomach tight with frustration.

Changing a pushy, demanding, and critical attitude is possible when we are willing to look at our
deeper needs. Most of these we can satisfy all by ourselves. And when we need another's help, simply asking for it exercises our humility and reminds us we're
not alone.

*Today, let me realize that the way to love is through
giving and requesting instead of demanding.*

April 29

If you treat man as he appears to be, you make him worse than he is. But if you treat man as if he already were what he potentially could be, you make him what he should be.

Johann Wolfgang von Goethe

The man or woman who delights in, recognizes, and encourages the best in others is a joy to experience. Perhaps there is no finer gift than the ability to sincerely validate another person.

There is always something good to be found in another. We are often in need of personal connection and affirmation and there are many critics in life, but few celebrators. Celebrators are those special people who can, with a word or a touch, affirm the worth of another. Wouldn't we rather add to the beauty and joy of the world than subtract from it?

When we celebrate the worth of others we make our own energy and electricity. The people who know us will want to stand in our light to have their goodness exposed, and we will find ourselves surrounded by friends who bring us their best.

Today, let me practice being a celebrator of the goodness and worth of others.

*We are utterly powerless to offer ourselves
or those we love protection . . . from our
necessary losses.*

   Judith Viorst

   We all travel a journey of letting go and moving on
to different people, places, and things. The older we
get, the more we realize we can't always expect life to
go our way or to keep on going the same way without
change. Facing disappointments and accepting the
reality of what we don't get is part of life. It isn't easy
to grieve and accept our "necessary losses."

   When we look back over our years we can begin
to see a tapestry that makes more sense now than it did
when we were going through it. Yes, there is a meaningful and lovely pattern to the big picture. This
knowledge of an overall rightness of our direction
helps us face the coming years more wisely. We now
find that we are surviving life pretty well in spite of
ourselves and are starting to relax enough to let in
some joy. We are beginning to see tomorrow more as
an advantage than a trial.

*Today, let me understand the freedom I will get as I
accept the concept of necessary losses.*

May 1

There is an abundance of beauty and joy in each day and the "detectives of life" find it.

Theresa Goodwill

We have some peak days when everything goes our way and we feel exhilarated, especially gifted in our lives. Peak days seem to be our special blessings whose effects help us make it through more routine times. Someone once said that on most days we put one foot in front of another and "do the daily dishes of living."

But we can find joy and discovery in our ordinary days, too. When we do this, we'll find that learning to enjoy and relish our average day brings us many gifts. We find that it is the joys in small pleasures that are most rewarding. Peak experiences are uplifting and wondrous, but they are not the essence of life. Appreciation of the commonplace fills us up with an easy peace and steady balance that makes putting our feet on the floor in the morning a happy task.

Today, let me identify and cherish the commonplace happenings of my average day.

*Intimacy means trusting that our friends
will see our virtues as foreground, our vices
as blur.*

Judith Viorst

Close friendship requires joyful interest in the other person, a firm commitment, and a listening ear. It also requires forgiveness and tolerance of the shadow side of our friend. It is a sharing of light and shadow with another in safety.

Intimacy is never a judge or scorekeeper in another's life. Instead it is a mediator and giver of absolution. We have learned in our own lives that most of us are extremely hard on ourselves—in fact we are our own worst critics. With this in mind, we are able to more clearly see the right task of loving friendships. When we take the risk to get close to another we have a wonderful opportunity. When someone opens up and becomes vulnerable to us, we can then sow the seeds of understanding and forgiveness in the most barren fields of their lives. In doing so, we not only give and nurture love, we prepare a structure of support for ourselves when we might need someone else's friendly ear and caring advice.

Today, let me focus on the good in my friends and loved ones, remembering that they have no need for my criticism.

May 3

Discouragement is a kind of retreat where we can escape reality and soothe ourselves in self-pity.

Norman Vincent Peale

Nothing is so bad that it's worth the price we pay to sit on the "pity pot." Self-pity is seductive company. At first, we may seem to enjoy feeling sorry for ourselves. It seems to feel good to sink into the depth of the "poor me's." We can enjoy feeling self-righteous when we feel "nobody really understands us, or that we get all the bad breaks. We have found that self-pity is our own personal traitor. Just when we feel we've gotten comfortable with self-pity, it stops working for us.

People soon get tired of us and they stop paying us the attention we feel we deserve. We get tired of ourselves and self-pity becomes a coat that seems too heavy to take off alone. It spoils our day and we usually end up feeling worse than when we started.

Living in the health of today means taking a firm stand about not being a victim. It means choosing consciously to use our power to make things happen for us, not to us.

Today, let me know my strength and use it in one small way.

*Release love into every situation and see
what happens.*

        Eileen Caddy

Some say love and fear are our two most primary emotions. We can choose to live in a fear-focused or love-focused reality. We might say we have no choice, that life gives us loving or fearful situations to respond to. It's true that we don't deal life's cards, but it is also true that we have a choice about the cards we wish to keep and those we decide to toss out. Believing we are powerless and that life is stacked against us will keep us in the lap of fear.

Fear and love are both powerful emotions that are recharged at opposite ends of our energy fields. Fear takes a lot of our energy, and love returns our energy in abundance. Many of us who have lived fear-focused lives have a hard time switching on the light of love. We are finding that the first step towards love is to learn to let go of fear. This might seem like a big order, but people all over the world are finding creative and spiritual ways to release fear and replace it with trust and love. No matter how many years we have carried the burden of fear, it is possible to begin to lay it down today.

Today, let me let go of one fearful thing and replace it with one loving thing.

May 5

*Failure is God's own tool for carving some
of the finest outlines in the character of His
children.*

Thomas Hodgkin

Fear of failure has been a painful companion for
many of us. It sits on the sidelines watching for us to
goof up. And so we do. Life is about goofing up,
learning, and not being perfect. Many of us got early
messages about the value of doing things "right." We
learned to connect our self-esteem with our accomplishments and we have an almost impossible time forgiving ourselves for making human mistakes.

This burden of striving for perfection and, in our
own eyes, never being quite good enough, has worn us
out. Perhaps now we may be willing to retire our yard-
sticks of perfection. Accepting that we sometimes fail
and are still good and worthwhile persons is an experience in self-forgiveness. Suddenly we find ourselves
feeling more mellow and less judgmental. Being able
to accept our humanity frees us to jump into life and
take risks, accepting our failings as part of life's plan.

*Today, let me realize that my value is not connected to
my successes and failures, but instead to my innate
worth as a child of God and of the universe.*

*People who face up to their age won't expect
their bodies to run smoothly over forty
without help, any more than one would
expect to prize an antique car for its hand-
some patina without constant maintenance
and frequent tune-ups.*

                    Gail Sheehy

Personal self-care is the mark of maturity. The
practice of caring for ourselves demonstrates our
acceptance of the aging process. There comes a day
when we accept as real the wrinkles and sags in the
mirror. The day when we claim the gray hair in the
mirror as our own is the day we may begin to relax
into our reality. We don't have to choose to accept that
our hair will remain gray, but it is important that
we really experience that person in the mirror as
ourselves.

Accepting that our bodies are aging frees us to
care for ourselves in loving, nurturing ways. We begin
to accept that we may need more than once-a-year
dental and medical check-ups. We learn we can be
physically active but we don't have to be the winner in
every race. An afternoon nap becomes a refreshing
break instead of a geriatric defeat.

As we learn to take good care of ourselves, we
view this as wisdom instead of weakness. In our age
we learn acceptance as well as feel the renewed hope
and discovery of new visions and directions.

*Today, let me learn to age with grace as I accept the
special needs of my body and spirit.*

May 7

Zest is the secret of all beauty.
    Christian Dior

The heart of true beauty is not found in physical appearances but instead in the light behind the physical. We have all met people who, according to the standards of fashion and the times, were not attractive. But when they entered a room everyone focused on their radiance and energy. Beauty in its most vivid form is something that flows from and surrounds a person in light. It is a zestful energy that is magnetic in its reality and connection.

Some people seem to have a certain love for living that erupts in their simple daily communications. They might be awed by a flower or enthralled by a windstorm and everyone they meet feels as if they are sincerely welcomed.

These people seem to shine out toward others, to be living life instead of being self-involved. Perhaps that is the truest form of beauty—the availability and openness to other human beings that says we are all celebrations.

Our beauty will never fade if we trust ourselves to genuinely experience the loveliness of others as we meet them.

Today, let me meet life with open arms.

*If you observe a really happy man you will
find him building a boat, writing a symphony, educating his son, growing double
dahlias in his garden, or looking for dino-
saur eggs in the Gobi desert.*

    Beran Wolfe

There is a certain happy energy that comes from
following our heart's desires. It is the feeling of contri-
bution and involvement in the use of our gifts that
make us feel best about ourselves.

Geese have an instinctive sense of their special
destiny and direction, and their flight is joyous in its
freedom. When we are using our deepest gifts and
responding to an activity or creation that feels right,
we too seem to soar. When we hit on the right challenge, we become inspired and invigorated. It feels as
if we have a way to put our special stamp on life.

Listening to our hearts and instincts will direct us
along the path that is just right for us. Once we have
experienced the joy of using our right gift we will fight
to keep it in our lives; it becomes the air our spirits
breathe.

Our special reality might be anything from fly-
casting to playing the dulcimer. It might bring us quiet
peace or the admiration of many people. It always fills
that space inside us that is of our spirits, the space that
is meant to be filled by our own hands.

*Today, let me unearth my special blessing, an activity
that I become so involved in that I lose track of time.*

May 9

The basic fact of today is the tremendous pace of change in human life.

   Jawaharlal Nehru

There is a story about a woman who had lived in many houses and cities in her life. She longed for one last place to settle into and call home, but this didn't seem possible for quite a while. Thinking about another necessary move put her into a panic. She had always been a resourceful person and had weathered many storms in good humor, but now she was beginning to feel limited by a newly-developed fear. She spoke to her spiritual advisor about her fear and resistance to more change. The burden was lifted when her advisor simply said, "Don't be fearful, don't you know you have the resources to move fifty more times if necessary?" Fear changed to strength when the troubled woman was reminded of her strength and resources.

When we choose to focus on abundance instead of lack we lose our paralyzing fear of change. We can't predict the course life will set for us, but we can nurture our power and resources to meet it as a changing and friendly teacher instead of an enemy.

Today, let me concentrate on the abundance of my resources.

*Here is the test to find whether your mission
on earth is finished: If you're alive it isn't!*
　　Richard Bach

Every one of us has a purpose in life. There is no
such thing as an empty, purposeless moment in time.
Often, when we are going through hard times, it's hard
to stand back and find rhyme or reason for our troubles. As our lives move on, we are slowly discovering
how time is our teacher. It is only in mid-life that we
have begun to value the wisdom we are discovering in
seeing the big picture. When we look back over our
lives, we begin to make beautiful sense out of the plots
of our misadventures. It is amazing how much sense it
all makes when we have a broader perspective.

A wonderful sense of safety, purpose, and comfort is ours when we begin to see our experiences as
necessary teachers directed toward our goodness and
best interest.

Choosing to view our lives as a mission instead of
an accident is liberating and awe-inspiring. Suddenly
we begin to take less for granted and look more deeply
into our difficulties to find a friendlier meaning.

*Today, let me celebrate the ongoing purpose and plan
of my life.*

May 11

In the old days, if a person missed the stage-coach, he was content to wait a day or two for the next one. Nowadays we feel frustrated if we miss one section of a revolving door.

Doris Dolphin

We would like to slow down and become quieter, but our restlessness will not allow it. Our lives seem filled with movement and frantic activity without end, as if this were our sole route to happiness as human beings.

At the same time, we know we need harmony and peace, tranquility, order, and meaning as we grow older.

When we find ourselves too active, sometimes we feel that we are somehow deceiving ourselves. Yet the mere thought of a calmer existence devoted to serious reflection is contrary to our modern way of life that we resist it.

As long as we seek meaning in life from some external source, we will continue to be frustrated. When we enter into silence, when we risk sitting in a chair and looking out the window or driving without the radio on, we may feel anxious. But silence can reacquaint us with our older, wiser selves—selves long drowned out by noise from within and without who can answer our suffering with words that make sense.

Today, let me continue this journey without a map, as I seek to find my way of wisdom.

The older we get the more we need to play.
Maurice Lovelace

Learning how to play again is a prescription often written for stressed-out forty- and fifty-year-olds. It is a natural tranquilizer for emotion and physical overload. When we ride a bicycle for example, we not only reap the benefits of aerobic exercise but feel the healing breath of the wind.

When is the last time we played a team sport like volleyball or engaged in a game of ping-pong? Remember sitting or squatting down on the ground to play marbles or jacks? Remember swinging on a swing set or from a tire, blowing bubbles, playing tiddley winks, playing monopoly?

The possibilities of play end only with our imaginations. Taking off our "adults shouldn't act this way" hats may be uncomfortable at first. We might feel silly if we haven't played in a long time. But it all comes back once we take the first step. Like riding a bike, we never forget how.

For help and instruction, here's where we can look to children, our own or others. They can remind us what our culture would have us forget. They can help us wake up the child within who still longs to play.

Today, let me relearn the joy of play.

May 13

All of a sudden, I was alone each day with the swimming goldfish and ticking of the clock.

Ruth Willow

Active parenting is a role that ends too abruptly for many of us. What happens to our lives when our children leave home? For years we have made our mothering and fathering central to our living and loving. Stunned, we may find ourselves missing the Little League games and chauffeuring we complained about. No more Girl Scout cookies to help deliver, tooth fairy money to place under a pillow, or curfew time and report cards to argue about. No one prepared us for the emptiness of neat, vacant bedrooms and the peace and quiet we used to long for. The real emptiness seems to be inside us. Who and what do we dream for now? How do we switch attention back to our own lives and marriage?

The grief of our empty nest is part of a process that brings eventual healing and reconnection to ourselves. We need to nurture and be especially gentle to ourselves before and during "letting go" times, grateful that we are able to give our children wings. It may help to know that we're also getting new wings of our own. No longer are we tied by our own apron strings to our children. We can now reclaim a large part of our lives for ourselves alone.

Today, let me believe that there is life after children.

> *Working outdoors, John maintains what I*
> *call a celestial connection, and, like*
> *patients in the hospital who have been*
> *known to heal faster when their room has a*
> *view of the sky, he is healthier because of it.*
>
> *Bernie S. Siegel*

Sunshine, air, and wind are healing elements. They are nature's free medicine that helps us get better when we feel physically and emotionally sick. It is hard to stay depressed when we are looking up at the sky. People who joyously live next to the soil and earth seem more grounded in life.

Getting out into the air and sunshine is often the best medicine for us. Some of us crave light and sunshine so much that we actually get depressed during the dark days of winter. Taking a walk in the open air and really looking at the glorious world around us will lift our tired hearts and bodies and encourage our healing. It gives us exercise for the body, stimulation for the mind, and refreshment for the spirit. When we return to our home we bring with us the connections we've just made with and nature. Thus, we not only relieve ourselves of old burdens, but we carry a new message of light and grace and spiritual connection to everything we do.

Today, let me really look at the miracles of air, wind, sunshine, and water, and see them as my healer.

*Humor is a prelude to faith and laughter is
the beginning of prayer.*

Reinhold Niebuhr

Laughter is a natural healer. Laughter exercises the lungs, stimulates the circulatory system, and exercises our breathing muscles. It increases oxygen in the blood. It has been scientifically proven that laughter induces relaxation and helps control pain. Laughter increases the production of endorphins, the body's natural painkillers.

We all have a natural capacity for humor and laughter that can be developed and increased at any age. Laughter is the "great let go" and we hardly ever feel better than after a good belly laugh.

The happiest kind of humor is that which makes light of life and its many contradictions and change without our laughter being at the expense of another person.

In listening to people with positive attitudes who have survived life's storms, you will often hear them say, "My humor saved me." Humor and laughter will continue to be our saving grace in a sometimes ungraceful world. It is something to be cherished and celebrated regularly with other good-humored folks.

Today, let me be able to really let go and laugh from the tips of my toes to the top of my head.

*When I dwell for any length of time on my
own shortcomings, they gradually begin to
seem mild, harmless, rather engaging little
things . . . .*

Margaret Halsey

When we sense that our flaws are interfering with
our progress toward self-fulfillment, we can take an
inventory of them. To recognize our shortcomings
without passing judgment on ourselves takes practice
and courage.

Making changes in ourselves, however, requires
still more patience, help, consistent effort, and gutsy
determination. Behaviors or traits we now perceive to
be shortcomings once enabled us to survive. Though
they've outlived their usefulness, they can't be completely uprooted overnight.

We can start by not blaming others for what we
find we've become. We own ourselves, warts and all.
This admission frees us to be human. It frees all the
energy we expend on denial. And it frees all the time
we spend touching up our masks of perfection. We
don't need to wear so much makeup anymore.

All this freeing up of time and energy makes
room for the courage and stamina we need to continue. And in continuing we connect with the power
we have to change our lives because we are no longer
blaming them on others.

*Today, let me acknowledge my faults and neither make
excuses nor indict others for them.*

*No longer say "yes" when you really want
to say "no." Your inner powers will make
your success certain.*

Vernon Howard

Saying yes while our insides scream no is the
maker of heart attacks, high blood pressure, ulcers,
depression, panic attacks, resentments, and a host of
other physical and emotional illnesses. When our
mouths lie, our bodies and emotions tell the truth
for us.

For many of us, people-pleasing and caretaking at
the expense of our own wishes and needs is reflexive.
We learned growing up that good little boys and girls
take care of others first. We learned that it is a selfish
child who thinks of him or herself.

The older we got, the more our own needs popped
up and the more guilt, confusion, and anger we felt
while walking the high wire between caring for ourselves and others. Sooner or later our bodies and emotions rebelled and challenged us to review our
priorities.

Is it really doing others a favor to say yes to others
all the time when our own needs get lost? Is it honest to
say yes when we want to say no?

Coming to terms with our own needs and values
has begun to give us the courage to reply to others
with an honest voice, and the good news is that we are
healthier.

*Today, let me have the courage to be honest with others
about what I feel is right for me.*

That best portion of a good man's life are
His little, nameless, unremembered acts of
kindness and love.

William Wordsworth

Kindness is the key that connects us to each other. Everyone deserves and needs kindness. Kindness given and received seems to validate us as human beings. But to be kind we must understand others and be empathetic. Unless we are willing to open our hearts and understand the pain of our friends and family, we will only be conditionally kind—giving or withholding on the basis of our own stern judgment.

Withholding kindness feels like a slap in the heart to another. Giving kindness means so much and costs so little. It is one gift we can easily give to others if we choose to do so.

Today, let me remember the value of unconditional kindness. Am I kind to all the people in my life?

May 19

*Trials are but lessons that you failed to
learn, present again.*

A Course in Miracles

Certain difficulties seem to repeat themselves over and over, just as certain types of people seem to enter and re-enter our lives. But the hardest situations and people can be our best teachers. When we trust enough to detach from our angry reactions, we are able to stand back and understand the lessons we are meant to learn.

Do we hold on to negative reactions? What purpose do these reactions serve in our life? What would we have to give up to let go of our old negative reactions? How do these people remind us of ourselves? What lesson can we learn about ourselves in this situation?

Often, just understanding why we act as we do helps us to change. Answering these questions honestly takes courage, but the results can free us. When we let any person or situation control our reactions, we give our power and freedom away. Realizing we can change only our own attitude is the foundation for happy living.

Today, let me have the courage to learn from my difficult life "teachers."

The way out is via the door: How is it that no one will use this method?

Confucious

We may complicate life by too much thinking, fixing, controlling and worrying. Life for many becomes a soap opera, and such a state of turmoil and crisis can become chronic.

Today we can choose to live in the problems in a solution. A simple way to change is to stop inviting crisis. What can we peacefully handle in one day's time? Perhaps this is the question we need to first ask ourselves. Do we have such a string of activity that there is little room left for peace, quiet, relaxation, and clear decision-making?

Weeding the busy gardens of our life will allow the flowers of peace and simplicity to grow, and gives us better time to nourish what is important and in need of attention in our hearts.

Today, let me unclutter my life and learn to focus on the simple things.

May 21

Find a point of love.

Charles Fillmore

It has been said that in every person and situation there is some point to love, and it is our challenge to find it. What about finding a point of love in ourselves each day? While we are learning to reach out and love others we may often neglect ourselves. It is by learning to accept and love our best and not fear our worst that we are uplifted.

Self-love is not selfish love, as we may have been taught. It is instead an act of humility. Humility is the ability to see and accept reality as it is. And the reality of life is that we are lovable and deserving of love.

If we refuse to accept that we are good, we will not be able to truly believe that others are. Thus it is that on our journey to others, we must begin with ourselves. Acknowledging and savoring our own worth lays the foundation for harmonious daily living and opens us up to the beauty in those around us.

Today, let me write a list of all the ways that I am a loveable and good person.

*Pain has an element of blank, it cannot
recollect when it began, or if there were a
day when it was not.*

Emily Dickinson

It has been said that living with pain makes saints
of ordinary men and women. When pain or illness lin-
gers, it feels as if an enemy has come into our lives
without invitation. Pain may become a constant companion or a frequent visitor who lurks around our door,
always ready to barge in on a moment's notice. When
we are living with chronic pain, we quickly learn that
we must find some way to make peace with this
enemy, otherwise it will quickly dominate our lives.

Learning to relax our physical and emotional
muscles can take some of the horror out of our suffering. When we resist and tighten up, our agony wors-
ens. Learning how to breathe deeply and lean into our
pain will quiet some of its raging force. Pain may be
likened to a river's current: we become more comfortable when we finally decide to flow with the current,
instead of against it. This relaxation, this surrender to
forces we can't control, also frees for us the power we
need to be involved in our own healing.

Today, let me learn how to conquer pain and fear.

Don't try to force anything. Let life be a deep let go. See God opening millions of flowers every day without forcing the buds.

Bhagwan Shree Rajneesh

By forcing life, we end up in opposition to living. We can cooperate with the flow of time and gently ride its winds, or we can get old and gray before our day by moving against the eye of the storm. We're finding we are no competition for life. If we meet it as friend, we win—although not always by our blueprint.

The more we learn of living, the more we feel, sense, smell, and taste a purposeful rhythm to all existence. In mid-life we have painfully and joyfully come to accept that we are not in charge. We can and do make decisions and choices, but life takes us, we do not take it. A kind of graceful protection carries us through to days and times, lands and shores, lovers and friends, that we never dreamed or imagined.

Getting out of the driver's seat of life and trusting that we will be perfectly taken care of is the easiest and hardest of life's lessons, all rolled into one.

Today, let me let go and become a participant in life. Help me stop trying to move life, and let life move me.

We cannot teach the dying how to die. If we are there, however and if we are paying attention, they will teach us.

> *Judith Viorst*

People who are dying will tell us what they need, if we learn to listen. We all live differently and we choose to die in our own way. Some of us will want to have the medical security of a hospital; others would prefer to die at home in a favorite room with family around.

Sometimes we need to listen to what the dying don't say, as well as what they are saying. It may be our need—not theirs—to focus on last rite wishes and instructions. We may want people to visit them whom they have no interest in seeing. We can look closely, observing body language and facial expressions. We can ask, "What do you really want?" And we can listen to the answers.

We may need to take some time and determine what are our own personal needs, and what the dying person seems to want. Listening with a third ear during our own grief is one of the best gifts we may give someone we love.

Today, let me listen with my heart and respect another's wishes even if they differ from mine.

May 25

Your disability is your opportunity.
    Kurt Hahn

Identifying our most serious personality shortcoming takes a lot of guts. And making a decision to change this shortcoming is a true act of courage. It seems easy for us to work on the edge of our problem areas, but stepping into the middle of our own personal hornet's nest is usually another story. Our most troublesome shortcoming is usually the one hardest to recognize, accept, and let go.

Perhaps we are plagued by jealousy and possessiveness of those we love. Or we may be eaten up with envy and resentment. Whatever our worst problem, it seems to rear its ugly head at the worst times, causing us and others much pain.

Making a decision to get rigorously honest about all our shortcomings can be a great relief. We discover that the more courage we have in doing our personal housecleaning, the greater will be our opportunity to grow and change. It's never too late to be better.

Today, let me be brave enough to take a deep look inside and make some honest decisions about change.

If we could read the secret history of our enemies, we would find in each man's life sorrow and suffering enough to disarm all hostility.

Henry Wadsworth Longfellow

If for one minute we were to link hands around the globe and feel the likeness of our humanity, we would never again be the same.

In looking into the hearts and eyes of each other, we would see our lives reflected back. The circumstances would be different, but our fears, dreams, and hurts would be the same. When we reach out to harm another, we would come to understand that we are in fact hurting ourselves and future generations.

There is a bond created by the sameness of humanity that, if understood could light fires of compassion around the world. We are more alike than we are different. In that fact lies the hope of communication and eventual global understanding. And let us not forget that it is as important to this understanding that we reach out to a nearby neighbor as it is to do so with someone halfway around the globe. Our journey of peace must begin with a single step. This is not the pipedream of a few, but a power that can change the world.

Today, let me do my part to light a fire of compassion, believing that one day there will be enough fires lit to allow us to really see each other.

All of our lives have led us to "Now," this moment in time. We are exactly where we are supposed to be.

Mary Rice

What does it really mean to live "one day at a time?" Is living in today an emotional or an intellectual experience? Our head can tell us that it's a good idea to focus on twenty-four hours at a time, but without our heart's permission, can we take the bold leap into the reality of now?

Projecting and frantic worry about the future, mixed with a dose of past regrets, can actually make us heartsick. Life becomes merely a survival experience when we carry the burdens of yesterday, today, and tomorrow on our backs, and sooner or later we will break down. Pain and desperation force us to make some necessary decisions about what we can safely put into our pack each morning. Do we have room for regret and resentment? Or should we fill the day with happiness and forgiveness?

The choice is ours. Choosing to live with our hearts in the minutes and hours of today is the finest gift of freedom and self-love we can give ourselves.

Today, let me honestly examine the advantages and disadvantages of living in the now.

Courage is almost a contradiction in terms.
It means a strong desire to live taking the
form of a readiness to die.

G.K. Chesterton

By surrendering to life we begin to accept our death, and we cease to struggle with trivial matters. Learning to fully live challenges us to fully accept dying. This acceptance is not passive. It means we step right into the middle of our fears and problems, not avoiding any dark corners. When we face the facts of life it has an interesting result. The more we are able to confront our worst fears, the tamer they become, and the calmer and more assured we are. Life becomes easier to live.

We will always be handed problems, but the more we trust our resources, the braver we get. Sooner or later we will probably choose to look at the big picture and let go of the people, places, and situations we can't change. In this letting go we find our true freedom to live fully and to courageously risk sharing this fullness with others.

Today, let me claim the joy in living that comes with having the courage to face my fears.

May 29

*There are some days when I think I'm going
to die from an overdose of satisfaction.*

Salvador Dali

Learning to accept joy is a lesson we may have overlooked all our lives. For many of us, life has been more drudgery than joy, and we don't expect to be happy. As we have worked and grown through the ups-and-downs of our lives, we have already left behind a lot of old emotional garbage, grief, and loss. Yet, accustomed as we may be to problems and misery, it may be difficult to put on our new coat of joy. It looks and feels so pretty and bright, but we question if it is really ours. Do we deserve to have something so beautiful?

In growing healthier, we find that we have been given the gifts of appreciation and gratitude and we begin to actually feel happy most days. We also have begun to accept ourselves, to enjoy better self-esteem, and to look at our true accomplishments with awe.

Adjusting to happiness means learning to accept the fruits of our labors and struggles. Gradually our new happy garment begins to feel comfortable and real to us. It is a beautiful day for us and others when we accept that this new coat is really ours and it won't be taken away.

Today, let me realize that I deserve joy and happiness.

Just when you've settled for being an ordinary person, you find out you're a super person, because a grandchild comes along who holds that opinion.
Phyllis Diller

One of the bonuses of mid-life is the arrival of a new generation—our grandchildren. Although each newborn shares direct genetic links with two parents and three other grandparents, our bloodline is in there, too. The heritage of all our ancestors becomes embodied in this new life! We have every right to participate in the joy.

When we feel a twinkle of recognition, a familiar gesture or a feature we know instinctively belongs to us, we remember the older generation more kindly. We can feel ourselves as a significant part of the extended family for these new ones. Amid our grandchildren, we find our hearts opened and our love multiplied. We are about to play a very important role in the lives of these young ones as givers of unconditional love and approval.

Today, let me glow with the new hope I've been given through the presence of my grandchild.

I'd much rather be having fun in the bed-room instead of doing all this talking in the living room.

　　　　　Elizabeth Ray

It is easy to overreact when it comes to our sexuality. We hold our sex lives as intensely personal and private. Yet the reality of our sexuality speaks volumes about us.

Dissatisfaction with our sexual being is, at mid-life, more often a symptom of other issues: power struggles, the need for a quick fix, boredom, physical problems, or distortions of our personal image.

A loving sexual relationship requires our constant attention if it is to thrive. Can we try treating our sexual partner as our best friend, with the utmost trust? Can we accept ourselves as lovable beings? Can we really believe we have a right to a happy relationship with our physical selves?

In mid-life, we have the maturity, wisdom and resources to change when we need to. A more satisfying, joyous life can be ours. When we honestly face who we are and compare this with who we want to be. By expressing our true selves sexually we can take a great stride in bringing our dream of ourselves into reality.

Today, let me cherish the sexuality unique to me.

*If I had my life to live over again, I should
form the habit of nightly composing myself
to thoughts of death. There is no other practice which so intensifies life.*

Muriel Spark

Fears of our own death may keep us uncomfortable and on edge throughout our lifetime. Viewing
death as the enemy instead of a transition and part of
the life process keeps us living in dread of what might
happen tomorrow.

We had no conscious choice about our birth, but
we have a lifetime to make peace with our death. It has
been suggested that the best time to think about death
is when we are feeling well and healthy. Some of us
have felt that by not even thinking about death we
could somehow magically protect ourselves. But we
found that in making death a fearsome, whispered
subject, we only added to our fear and robbed ourselves of fully enjoying today.

Few of us want to die, but all of us will. Death is
as much a part of life as birth is. It is, in fact, our right,
our challenge, and the backdrop against which we can
attain glory. When we make peace with our physical
mortality, we are free to better enjoy our todays and
our tomorrows.

*Today, let me live in the sunshine of knowing that
death will no longer hold me a fearful captive.*

June 2

*I will really be free . . . when I learn to
speak up for me without harming thee.*

Sue Stenberg

Assertive behavior is compassionate behavior. It is caring enough about ourselves and others to learn to speak our feelings directly without being defensive or attacking others.

Assertive rights include the right to express our feelings, to say "no" to others, to make mistakes, to change our minds, to set our own priorities in life, to be treated with dignity and respect, to take responsibility for ourselves, and to be "illogical" in making personal decisions.

Learning to be directly assertive is a valuable communication skill that takes practice. Many of us have learned to express ourselves by being aggressive or assaultive. Then we wondered why others responded to us defensively.

By being clearly assertive about our feelings we let others into our world. They come to know us, to see our honesty, and to trust it. And we gain the freedom to live by our own values, guided by our own heart.

Today, let me honestly express myself to another.

I could spend 80 hours a week at work.
But there's more to life than that. If I have
to settle for a little less money or status, it's
worth it.

Alan Mason

When our co-worker in the next office dies suddenly at a young age, we are shocked into asking, "Could this happen to me?"

Medically we may be healthy specimens, but what about the rest of our existence? Are we serene? Do we take time for ourselves? The lure of working long hours will always be present: incessant deadlines must be met, employer expectations to which we "can't" say no, the promise of more money, our name in important places, the next promotion.

It may be time to think about what we really want in life. Do we want success or serenity, recognition or contentment?

If another's misfortune prompts us to rethink our intensity and long hours on the job, then that death has not been in vain. We can change and begin to rediscover our real values while we still have time. And the wonderful thing about change is, it can start now, with just one small act.

Today, let me leave work early and see if the world comes to an end.

June 4

Suffering isn't ennobling, recovery is.
   Christiaan N. Barnard

Putting a bandage on a wound over and over again will not end the pain nor cure the sore. The pills, drinks, binges, escapes, running away, changing partners, geographic changes: these are some of the bandages we've used to treat our problems. But if the wound keeps reopening and causing anguish repeatedly through the years, we need to gather courage and look for the right doctor, take the new medicine, and find true recovery rather than continue looking for the quick fix.

When we see that the only good medicine comes from within, and that, with the help of our Higher Power we can recognize the true source of our pain, we begin to heal. This is true recovery, and it comes from the inside out.

Today, let me find the courage to let go of pain and change.

*The writer shakes up the familiar scene,
and as if by magic, we see a new meaning
in it.*

> *Anais Nin*

Mid-life is a good time to consider what we'd say
were we to write an autobiography. If our book has ten
chapters, the first five or six can be written; those
parts of our lives have been completed.

It gives us a helpful perspective sometimes to
review past events, rearrange the memories, and recall
old feelings, now that we've established some distance
from them.

When our children ask about grandparents who
died when they were too young to remember, what do
we tell them? Where are our roots, and what do they
mean to us now?

Mid-life is a time to outline the rest of our book.
How will our children speak of us to their children
when we're gone? Let us take time now to live out our
lives in a way that makes us proud and serene. Our
final chapters can be filled with joy and adventure,
integrity and love.

*Today, let me search for a fresh perspective on my past
and present.*

June 6

> . . . *60-year-olds should not be taken off*
> *and shot but should be revered, heeded and*
> *even cheered for having made it this far in*
> *one piece.*
>
> *Larry L. King*

Our movement through life is natural and inevitable. There can be rewards during each stage, and only small regrets as we slide form one into another.

Age is relative, and at mid-life we're more aware of that than ever before. We sense that our contemporaries do not feel their age internally, but feel all ages, and timeless. We can have both the joy of youth and the wisdom of maturity.

We have active choices to use our remaining years to the best of our abilities. Now there may be a bit more of a sense of urgency; our concept of time as well as age is shifting. But we know the value of a year, a month, a week, a day. And we've learned that for every loss due to age we gain far more in return.

Today, let me live this day with hope and purpose and a new healthy appreciation of time.

*It is my stronger belief that each person is
doing the very best that they can at this
moment in time.*

                    Sam Friend

Sometimes we choose to stay in relationships and
marriages that aren't good for us. That is a choice—
our choice—and we can also choose to beat ourselves
up for this decision, or work at accepting where we are
today as a necessary step in our growth. Until we are
ready to change a situation, it does us little good to feel
ashamed because we are involved in it. Believing that
we are exactly where we're supposed to be at this
moment in time will help us relax and not be so hard
on ourselves.

Change is a process; it doesn't happen overnight.
Relationship decisions are usually not easy or clear-
cut. Trusting our own willingness to be true to ourselves and to make good decisions is a most valuable
lesson in self-love. Intellectually, we may know we
need to leave a painful relationship, but we may need
more time to commit ourselves emotionally to this
step before we can act.

Taking small steps, putting one foot in front of the
other, is sometimes the best effort we can make.

*Today, help me trust that I will be led on the right path
at the right time.*

June 8

We can choose to see the world through the window of love rather than the window of fear.

Dr. Gerald Jampolsky

Love is a window that filters out the worst in ourselves and others and highlights our best. Being a parent is an act of courage and love. It is a very real opportunity to practice active loving in circumstances that are often difficult. Our children bring both joy and challenges with them into our family and seem to test us endlessly. As they grow older, we may become dumping grounds and scapegoats for unresolved pain from the past, and we may be struck with feelings of awe, guilt, and helplessness at their anger and hurt.

There are many occasions that demand choices and decisions from us. How will we act in these situations? Will we become a part of the emotional drama that we are being invited to participate in, or will we become part of the solution and be challenged to find a way to care that doesn't involve a power struggle?

Learning to lovingly listen and acknowledge our children's anger is the best skill a parent can hope to have. And by consistently choosing to look for the best in our children and ourselves, and not to fear the worst, we will bring ourselves closer to a clear peace of conscience.

Today, let me believe that my role as a parent is a special gift that challenges me to learn more about my resources and ability to love.

I celebrate myself, and sing myself.
Walt Whitman

People-pleasing can be an exhausting job. "Good" people-pleasers even have guilty dreams about not doing enough for others.

But when we get an "A" in people-pleasing, we are usually getting an "F" in loving ourselves. It is impossible to care for ourselves when we are constantly focused on keeping everyone else happy. And love becomes a heavy burden when we neglect our own needs. Not caring for ourselves is unnatural, and our inner voices soon cry to be heard. Sooner or later these voices get nasty and find indirect, angry ways to get their needs met like lashing out and blaming others in reaction to our own emotional overload. We may also find ourselves getting sick with the flu, or suffering muscle aches or pinched nerves from the stress.

But celebrating ourselves can set us free. We can give ourselves care, praise, and love—the things we were seeking from others. In time, we discover there is enough to keep, and enough to give to others as well. We are worthy of love, and we can learn to love ourselves.

Today, let me understand that only by caring for myself will I have the energy and love to give to others.

June 10

The first of earthly blessings, independence.
Edward Gibbon

Dating in mid-life and beyond is a challenging experience that usually begins with questions: "Where do we meet nice people?" "How do I know when someone is trustworthy?" "Will others still find me attractive?"

Mid-life brings other complications to dating, too. If a past relationship has failed, we may feel especially vulnerable and exposed. When we are painfully aware of our "defects," the risk of forming new relationships can be frightening.

Feeling that we are deserving allows us to find creative new ways to meet interesting people. Loving ourselves helps us avoid desperately settling on the first person who shows us interest. We feel worthy of loving care.

Most important, accepting and loving ourselves brings us joy in our own company. We are fulfilled. Spending time with others is a happy event, and we find other people like us better, too, when we are not begging for attention. With self-love, we find we have choices at last.

Today, let me learn to love my own company and trust that healthy self-love makes me attractive to others.

*It is the province of knowledge to speak and
it is the privilege of wisdom to listen.*

Oliver Wendell Holmes

When we share openly and listen actively, we
unlock the connecting doors between ourselves and
others. When we are full of ourselves, we have no ears
for others. We can become so focused on being heard
and getting our time that we forget communication is a
two-way street. The more we "talk at" people, the less
satisfied we feel, the less we believe we are really
heard by others. The more we demand, the less we
seem to get.

Before we can change those patterns we need to
understand how we communicate. We can start by
asking questions of people we trust: How well do you
think I listen to others? Do I give my full attention to
others when they're talking? How well do I communicate myself, my feelings and ideas, to others? What
changes would you like me to make?

Sometimes we get unbalanced in our communication; we talk too much or listen too much. Getting honest about our strengths and shortcomings is the first
step in changing, and growing closer to others.

*Today, let me learn to listen and to share with others.
Teach me the joys of good honest, two-way talk.*

June 12

Summer afternoon—summer afternoon; to me those have always been the two most beautiful words in the English language.

Henry James

Low humming sounds and sun-baked hazy days lull us into the slowed pace of summertimes. When we were growing up nothing was more magic than summertime. The hot, sweet-smelling days seemed to stretch on forever then. Summer was play itself, a seemingly endless string of months to work off energy and dream about the possibilities of everything and anything. Long daylight hours gave us a world that seemed boundless in its capacity to soothe and delight.

Children know best how to settle down into the heart of summer, to let go in deep down ways, to simply "be" and enjoy.

How long has it been since we sat down with summer and let her envelop us with smells, sounds, and memories? Just sitting still outside on a summer night, getting reacquainted with the season, can make us feel like kids again.

Today, let me make the time to relax into a summer day in the way of childhood.

I am larger, better than I thought, I did not know I held so much goodness.

Walt Whitman

Finding fault with ourselves is habit-forming and drains our energy. Perhaps we believe that criticizing ourselves will make us change. Our lives can be like flower gardens full of blossoms when planted and tended with loving care. Negative thinking only adds weeds and decay to our garden.

There is something very sad about fault-finders. They never seem to get enough! Negativity breeds negativity and eventually leads to ill health and unhappiness.

Stopping our patterns of personal fault-finding can be the beginning of positive change. When we realize we are criticizing ourselves, we can focus instead on our positive traits and behaviors. We can give ourselves honest praise for our accomplishments, and comfort ourselves when we are unhappy. We can learn to cherish ourselves for the wonderful, growing people we are right now. Learning to claim and accept our basic goodness is healing and refreshing. And positive thinking is contagious. Soon self-love becomes a habit, and a joyful new way of life.

Today, let me remember that I can choose to dwell on my positive assets or negative defects. The choice is mine.

If ye have faith as a grain of mustard seed,
ye shall say unto this mountain, Remove
hence to yonder place; and it shall remove.

Matthew 17:20

Faith builds faith. The more we believe in life's possibilities, the more faith we gain. God made us as hollow vessels waiting to be filled to overflowing with abundant gifts.

Each of us has the spark of a unique destiny inside. This tiny flame leads us in a right direction if we trust its warmth. God has a special task for us to accomplish in our life. No one else could fulfill this wish exactly like us. At some point, we will know what it is that we have been asked to contribute to life. It may be as simple as building a cathedral or as grand as loving a child. Our task will challenge us and at times may seem impossible. But no matter how discouraged we get, we need to remember that we will be given the grace to complete our life work.

Faith can fill us when we are empty, and comfort us in sorrow. As long as our faith remains, we shall always have hope.

Today, let me trust God's unfolding plan for me, and know that I am being guided and directed every step of the way.

Give all to love: Obey thy heart . . .
 Ralph Waldo Emerson

Relationships are the proving ground of our maturity and serenity. Our vulnerability is exposed when we risk getting close to people. When we truly love, the "real" us emerges. How do we respond to the intimacy and struggles that good relationships experience? Do we know how to work through difficult times? Do we find ourselves escaping too soon or staying too long? Some of us continue insisting, that there must be a solution, even when it's become clear that the problems are too great.

Caring for someone else brings us many opportunities to learn. We are finding that time has made us more honest. We have learned the essential rightness in being true to our beliefs and values. And when we find that we are giving up important parts of ourselves to accommodate the needs of someone else, we are learning to run, not walk, to the nearest exit.

Listening to and respecting our hard-earned values are essential tools in measuring our relationships. Does this relationship add or subtract from my peace of mind? Perhaps this is the final question we are loving ourselves enough to ask.

Today, let me practice wisdom in developing relationships.

June 16

All thoughts, all passions, all delights,
Whatever stirs this mortal flame,
Are all but ministers of love,
And feed this sacred flame.

Samuel Coleridge

When we deny our angry feelings, we poison our love relationships. When we repress and avoid our anger, we walk around with it stuffed inside. Eventually it erupts in twisted and hurtful ways.

It is impossible to truly love someone without feeling angry at some time. Intimacy is not timid and passionless, but full of deep feelings and powerful energy. It takes a great love to throw anger out on the table when it arises.

Ulcers, burnt dinners, icy silence, sexual withdrawal are some of the disguises that unexpressed anger may wear. The danger of not sharing anger is great. It may get lost in the stockpile of old hurts and become monstrous and complicated beyond clear expression. Non-abusive, direct anger clears the air for deeper levels of love to breathe and flourish.

Today, let me honestly express anger in my love relationship.

*Much human suffering is related to the false
expectations that we are called to take each
other's loneliness away.*

        Henry Nouwen

Maturity asks that we be responsible to others.
We learn to keep our promises, arrive on time, and
generally become a person others can count on.

Being responsible for others is a much heavier
burden. It's like picking up two buckets of cement to
carry, ours and theirs. It is the feeling of being
weighed down by someone else's troubles, but being
powerless to let go and step out of the picture.
Unhealthy guilt can keep us stuck doing for others
what they should be doing for themselves.

There is a story about a mother who begged the
headmaster of her son's boarding school to wake him
in the morning, since he was such a heavy sleeper he
wouldn't hear the alarm. The headmaster wisely
refused her request, saying her son always heard the
alarm for the vacation train. Like that mother, we can
learn to let others take care of themselves while we
tend to the joyful business of being responsible for
ourselves.

*Today, let me focus on caring for myself while allowing
others the same dignity and space.*

June 18

*There is no ending to the ripple effect of
shared love and its well wishing.*
Ruth Williams

Agape is God's love that arises from abundance
and seeks nothing from its object. It is born of grace
and allows us to see with our hearts. It is our human
outpouring of connected empathy. It is reverence for
the vulnerable soul of another.

Agape is gratitude and delight in our own recognition of the humanness of our beloved. It is a radiating
commitment to appreciate, handle with care, and not
damage what our beloveds have bravely shown us of
themselves.

This trusting exposure of others' goodness and
humanness, and our recognition and respect of it,
plants the seeds of awe and gratitude, in which love
multiplies, flourishes, and grows into the flower of our
life.

*Today, help me believe that love will open every door
of my life if I give without expectations.*

*Make a painting in which every part of the
painting is of equal importance.*

        Chuck Close

If we were to leave a legacy for our children we
might wish them to enjoy life, laugh more and not be
as serious as we've been. We'd try to accept them
making some poor decisions but perhaps not taking as
long as us to realize their mistakes.

We would wish that they be gentle with themselves and others, learning the beauty of forgiveness.

We would further wish that: They be married to
their partner instead of their job. They start exercising
and eating well before age forty. They learn the difference between abusive and assertive anger. They realize
that people are more important than things. They
practice promptly saying "I'm sorry." They act more
like a grandparent than a parent with their own children. They be kind to themselves, knowing they are
beautiful exactly as they are this day. Most of all, we
hope they will not judge their parents too harshly,
trusting that we wanted to love them well.

Today, let me give my child the gift of my good wishes.

June 20

I've given up the truth for those I've tried to please . . . and now it's my turn.

   Diana Ross

Sacrificing our rights often results in letting other people mistreat us. We deny our own importance by saying yes when we really mean no. We may need to learn that we have the right to say no. We are not rejecting another person—simply refusing a request.

Some of us have become self-sacrificing people-pleasers by saying "yes, yes, yes" to everyone and everything. We have let other people, places, and things control our lives. We have allowed our personal freedom to be trampled on. We may actually have become numb to our own needs.

Self-sacrificing people-pleasers and caretakers don't do themselves—or others—a favor. Other people come to count on them and start to expect that they be the only givers in relationships.

People-pleasers are often angry on the inside. They would love to stamp their feet and say "no, no, no," but they are afraid. Then the anger comes out in unhealthy ways. They may even become physically or emotionally ill.

Learning to say no is an act of love and honesty. When we speak up and are true to our feelings, people know who we are and where we stand. We can get our needs met and feel like the valuable, unique beings we really are.

Today, let me learn the healthy art of saying no when it is in my best interest to do so.

*A pessimist is one who burns his bridges
before he gets to them.*

>   *Sidney Ascher*

A recent study determined that most human
thinking is negative. It seems most of us are quick to
be critical. Many of us have become experts at judging
others. At times, we even seem to get a sense of real
satisfaction from finding others' shortcomings.

But sooner or later the habit of looking at the
world through dark glasses begins to sour our attitude
toward life. We become negative and pessimistic, and
not much fun for others to be around. We may not even
enjoy our own company.

Luckily, we can break the habit with time and
patience. The first step is to be aware of our thinking
and to make the decision to change negatives to positives. We can look for at least one good thing in every
person, place, or situation we encounter. Practicing
this new attitude will bring amazing results. We find a
new sense of lightness and peace. The world is a
friendlier place, and other people become a source of
joy. We begin to like others and ourselves better. Our
sleep is soon sounder, and our days brighter. By being
positive, we begin to see the richness of the world in a
whole new way.

*Today, let me be willing to ask for help to have the will-
ingness to look for positives in myself and others.*

June 22

*I insist that men shall have the right to work
out their lives in their own way, always
allowing to others the right to work out their
lives in their own way, too.*

Giuseppe Garibaldi

Is there a secret place in our heart that still
believes we can control others and force them to
change? Do we find ourselves hanging onto the hope
that our lives will get better when others change and
do things our way? Or have we learned that the only
person we can change is ourselves?

We have the power to set limits on the hurtful
behavior of others. We have the right and responsibility to clearly let others know our limits. And when
someone continues to be hurtful to us, we can find a
way to step out of that person's circle of pain.

But in letting go of the need to change others, we
liberate ourselves. We are responsible for our own
lives, and are free to let other people be responsible for
themselves. This is a wonderful new freedom that will
greatly enrich our lives.

*Today, let me believe that trying to force changes on
someone else is a waste of life's energy. Help me to
change me.*

*Love alone is capable of uniting living
beings in such a way as to complete and
fulfill them, for it alone takes them and
joins them by what is deepest in themselves.*

Pierre Teilhard de Chardin

There is a part of us that longs to be shared with
another human being. It feels wonderful when someone else's heart touches ours. There is nothing that
makes our insides feel better than knowing we are
loved.

All our lives we have filled our hearts up with
searchings, feelings, and memories. This accumulation is the person we really are, the self we present to
our beloved. It is the best gift we can bring to someone
else. It is so lovely when a special person says, "I want
to really know all of you. Whether you think the parts
are good or bad, I want to learn about the real you."
The best kind of love gently walks through the gardens
and deserts of our past looking for flowers of courage.
We are all beautiful inside, and love focuses on our
beauty instead of our faults.

Today, let me find dignity in the lives of those I love.

Nothing changes if nothing changes.
　　　　Earnie Larsen

Repeating the same behavior over and over and expecting different results keeps us on a merry-go-round. Change asks that we do something different, and mid-life is the ideal time to do a personal housecleaning.

What about our decisions, habits, and attitudes makes us unhappy? What are we willing to change? Now is the time to rid ourselves of excess baggage we don't want to carry into tomorrow.

What have we been putting off until later? Sometimes change asks that we look deeper at our patterns. Is there a hidden satisfaction in being late? What's the payoff? Are we acting out some secret anger? What would we give up by being on time? What would it be like to focus on our own lives instead of the lives of our adult children? Why might we resist letting go of them?

Looking honestly at our resistance to change will help us clean our old slate and decide how we would like to be different. We can be who we want to be and we can begin changing this very moment. With a little thought and effort, our lives can be all we expected.

Today, let me have the courage to get off old self-defeating merry-go-rounds and begin to make my life the way I want it to be.

*Often the greatest challenge isn't learning to
love others. It's learning to let them love us.*
Melody Beattie

People who can accept love from others have
healthy self-esteem. We must be open and vulnerable
to let the love of a dear one flow into us. We are letting
go of control when we are on the receiving end of love.

Many people find it easier to give than receive
because they feel safer when they are in control and
focusing on someone else's needs. Admitting we need
love, and then letting ourselves receive it, is a statement of trust in ourselves and others.

If we find we're uncomfortable being loved and
nurtured, we could change those old attitudes about
ourselves. In our morning quiet times, we can begin
by affirming our goodness and worth and listing our
good qualities on paper if necessary.

We can be kinder to ourselves all through the day,
rewarding ourselves for our successes, and forgiving
ourselves when we don't live up to our expectations.
We can learn to be gentle with our fragile egos and
learn to nurture ourselves. Soon, we feel worthy of
love from ourselves and others.

*Today, let me know that great beauty is standing still
and being available to receive the love of others.*

*I'm telling you there's something far more
exciting, romantic, spine-tingling, and
satisfying than chemistry. It's when you've
been with someone for five years, ten years,
or forty years, and the passion is still
deepening.*

Nita Tucker

"Commitment" is a vital word in the language of love. It is the decision to stay with a loved person and work through the reality of day-to-day life. Committed relationships seem to shine in spite of budgets that don't balance, falling arches, rebellious teenagers, and burnt meatloafs.

Commitment is love made visible and demonstrated in daily giving. It is going to the store to get milk at midnight, watching a movie instead of the game, knowing what a special smile really means, and walking the dog in the rain. It is staying together during dry, unromantic spells, and resisting the urge to find out if "the grass is greener on the other side of the fence."

There are months when nothing seems to go right in our relationships, and holding on is all we can do. In these times we can look back and savor the durability of our relationship. There is a bonus of deepening gratitude and tenderness given to people who value their commitments.

Today, let me value and discover the blessings of a long-standing relationship.

*We are better than we know. If we can be
made to see it, maybe from now on we'll be
unwilling to settle for less.*

> *Anonymous*

We are wonderful, capable human beings worthy
of love and happiness. We are all works of God's art,
and each one of us is beautifully special. We all have
an individual gift to give the world that can't be
duplicated.

The problem is, we often don't believe it. We are
used to focusing on our negative qualities and often
become experts at putting ourselves down. We have a
hard time believing and accepting our own goodness
and gifts.

When we have a negative mental attitude, only
one person can change it—us. We have the power to
change our thinking if we want to. Sometimes we are
afraid to give up our negativity and hopelessness.
What do we get out of staying the way we are? What
are we afraid we'll lose if we change? This is a question we need to honestly ask ourselves. Negative thinking can become a comfortable habit. It takes courage
to risk becoming positive and hopeful, but a new world
awaits us when we accept the challenge.

*Today, let me begin to believe that I am better than
I know*

June 28

Human life has its laws one of which is, we
must use *things and* love *people.*

Fr. John Powell

People are the world's most precious resource. A
study of prisoners of war found that their most important survival necessity was to find a way to communicate with one another between cells.

The longer we live, the more we appreciate our
need for community and fellowship. The measure of
respect and compassion we feel for our fellows reflects
the love we have for ourselves. We are all connected in
our weaknesses and our strengths, and when we shut
others out of our lives, we retreat into a bubble of sepa-
rateness that weakens our vitality.

Hurt, disappointment, and pain in relationships
may cause us to withdraw and turn inward in order to
protect ourselves, but when we carry our pain into our
cocoons it grows into a bone-deep loneliness.

It is never too late to break out of our prison and
risk loving and trusting life and people again. Talking
to a caring person and airing our pain is a way to begin
our journey back to the living. And we begin this
beginning with a single statement: "I need to talk
to you."

Today, let me believe that there are "safe" people to
trust, that it's never too late to trust again.

*Don't be dismayed at goodbyes. A farewell
is necessary before you can meet again,
after moments or lifetimes.*

Richard Bach

Life is filled with tender goodbyes and new beginnings. Friendship is like a precious treasure box brimming with shared personal history. It is such a loss to say goodbye to a dear friend, especially ones we've grown to count on over the years.

But what comfort we get from seeing them again and again. When we sit down and catch up on things, we feel rejuvenated, reconnected. Perhaps the finest treasure to be found in our friendships is the feeling of unconditional acceptance, even after a long separation. We need to prove nothing; our only task is to speak our hearts and be ourselves.

It is indeed sad to say goodbye to such a friend, but do we ever really lose that type of love if we but keep in contact?

Today, let me remember that my good friends will never really leave me.

June 30

Never build a case against yourself.
   Norman Vincent Peale

Because we're afraid to fail we often build a negative case against ourselves. We can become so discouraged that we lose our energy. Negativity seems to
breed more negativity, and before long we stop worrying about failing because we've stopped trying to
reach our goals. Then we stay in the safe middle
ground. We're not afraid, but we always wonder what
would have happened.

Sometimes we take our personal drama one step
further and blame other people, places, and things for
our problems. This quicksand of self-pity will keep us
depressed and paralyzed. It is a trick we play on ourselves to keep us thinking the power in our lives comes
from outside us. But it doesn't.

It's never too late to change negative thinking and
to practice self-forgiveness. We can start by looking
for the good in ourselves and others. We can focus on
loving acts and thoughts and ignore those that hurt us.
We can learn that we are responsible for the joy and the
sorrow we find every day.

Today, let me build a positive case for myself.

Nothing is by chance.
    Eileen Caddy

Believing that we are exactly where we need to be at this moment gives us a peaceful heart. The difficult situations and people in our lives are here to be our teachers. This may be easy to say when we're not mired in those difficulties, but the only way we make troubles into teachers is by remembering this principle when it really counts—when we're wrestling with the problem. It has been said that there are no accidents in life, only divine coincidence.

A great burden is lifted when we become willing to flow with the tides of life instead of fighting them. When we acknowledge that we are on a guided and blessed path, we can let go of fear and worry and use our energies to live life to the fullest.

Today, let me live with joy in the sure and certain knowledge that I am exactly where I need to be.

July 2

*Let us thus praise you in the way you love
best, by shining on those around us. Let us
preach you . . . by our example.*

Mother Teresa's Prayer

Parents who live their own lives with joy and
integrity give their children and grandchildren a price-
less gift. Teaching and sharing our life experiences is
different from demanding that our offspring live life
our way. We need some necessary control over our
smaller children, but that diminishes in time, as children become adults. We have little control over our
teenagers, and zero control over our adult children.

We may try to tie our older sons and daughters to
us through guilt, money, or other forms of control, but
soon everyone feels angry, confused, and off balance.
And, in fact, children can always see through our
words to our behaviors, anyway, and this is what they
learn from.

Becoming happily and actively involved in our
lives is the best example of love we can bring to our
families. Seeing Mom and Dad enjoying themselves
lets adult children focus their energy on the necessary
task of living their own lives, making and learning
from their own mistakes, and celebrating each success
as theirs.

*Today, let me share life through my example, being
fully committed to my own personal growth.*

I must love the questions themselves . . .
like locked rooms, full of treasures to which
my blind and groping key does not yet fit.
>   *Alice Walker*

We have many questions and few solutions. We are sometimes faced with problems that seem to defy fixing. When an answer finally appears, we are not left to rest on our laurels as new questions and personal mysteries challenge us.

Happiness is really to be found flowing in between the lines of life, in the weaving of our day-to-day tapestry. When we learn the sweetness of yielding and non-resistance, we steady and enrich our travels.

It has been said that pain is not in the change but instead in the resistance to the change. Our life continues to be a series of ups and downs, questions, answers, and more questions. It is made up of change. When we resist change, we resist life itself. Learning to relax and enjoy the experience is the key to joy.

Today, let me know I am always protected and on a right course.

July 4

You are only the channel through which divine action takes place, and your treatment will be just the getting of yourself out of the way.

Emmet Fox

Life itself is a healing process. This magnificent belief requires us to accept that the world is basically friendly and directed toward our good. We are all healers with unique gifts who have something to contribute to life. Finding our vocational niche is a task that continues throughout our lives. We often know when we have found our right place because it feels like "coming home."

As we walk our life path, it seems as if our feet know the way. It is a sure and certain intuitive knowledge that we are where we should be. Sometimes the journey seems long. At times like that it helps to remember that the events and people we encounter along the way are our teachers. When we are open like this, we are always young, always growing. And getting to know and trust ourselves is the first step we take on our path to this work.

Today, help me to be patient as I learn to better trust myself and the world.

I can choose to make me more of what I
want from you . . . we shall be bigger
together.

George F. Simons

We are in trouble when we try to change others to please ourselves. Controlling family and friends is a no-win situation that causes them to turn away from us. Sometimes we expect those we love to "fill us up," to make up for something we didn't get in life. But if we have an empty hole inside, we will never be happy if we expect external things to fix us.

Do we want to be so lonely, bitter, and old, with expectations were so great, complaints so loud, and self-pity so evident that others walk around the block to avoid meeting us on the street?

There is in each of us a way out of the darkness and into light. We can choose to look inside ourselves for what we need. It is the only place we can ever hope to find it, so the sooner we make this choice, the better —for us and for those around us.

Today, let me realize that I am the only one responsible for my life and happiness.

July 6

People on second journeys repeatedly betray
a deep sense of loneliness. This loneliness
should eventually turn into the aloneness of
a quiet and integrated self-possession.

Gerald O'Collins

Second journeys end with a new and mature mid-life wisdom. This wisdom is born of accepting our limitations and essential solitude. It is the sure and certain knowledge that no one else will ever completely understand us.

At our mid-life junction we are faced with two alternatives: empowerment or victimization. We can make the rest of our life happen, or sit back and let life happen to us.

If we are contemplating resigning ourselves to accept passively whatever happens, we are really deciding to die. We might need to take a close look at our unresolved grief. What might frighten us about being alone?

Life is a chain of repeated acts of trust, of reaching out to find new hope again and again. We are not promised a ride free from bumps, but we do find that life brings us blessings if we continue to hang on and navigate.

Today, let me remember that I am the master of my fate.

Caretakers are baby-makers.
                    Monica Stone

Doing for our children what they could do for themselves keeps them dependent and angry. Children's main task during adolescence is to detach from their parents. Our main task as parents is to let them. After having devoted years of time and energy to the guidance and development of their lives, we might feel a natural resistance to letting go. After all, we think we know the best way for them to do things. We wonder why they insist on doing things their own way, and in their own time. Why do they seem to have to make the same mistakes we did?

At times we unconsciously keep our children tied to us by running interference for them in their lives. When we rescue them from the natural consequences of living, we can sabotage their task of claiming independence. And in this way, we also keep ourselves from growing independent of them and living our own lives. It isn't rare to find this change difficult. It is a natural part of all the changes we're going through now, and all we can do is our best—little by little, day by day.

Today, give me the courage to let go so my children can experience the natural consequences and rewards of their acts.

July 8

*The way we were treated as small children
is the way we treat ourselves the rest of our
life. And we often impose our most agonizing suffering upon ourselves.*

Alice Miller

Letting go of our identity as victims or martyrs
means, for some of us, letting go of some very real
power we have over others. For most women and some
men that means letting go of the only power we have.

If our stance in life is that of the victim, chances
are we were victimized when we were young. Being a
victim is how we survived. It was how we cared for
ourselves.

Today, dropping into the role of victim or martyr
may be painful to us. Perhaps we don't know how else
to cope. There are other ways to tap our personal
power and meet our needs. But to know them we must
first do the difficult work of connecting with the child
within ourselves and feeling what it was that made
him or her a victim in the first place.

We are equal to this task. Meanwhile we need not
judge ourselves when the victim in us shows his or her
face. It is giving us knowledge that can help us heal.

*Today, help me feel compassion for the child within me
who was the real victim.*

*Everything has different aspects. A tragedy
is considered a very negative event. But if
you wait and look from a different angle,
you'd eventually find some positive aspects.*

Tenzin Gyatso

We cannot have lived this long without having
knowing some tragedy. None of us is immune from
crime, fire, accidents, death. After the shock, terror,
and initial grief, we are often driven back against ourselves. We ask, why me? Or, why not me? Do I want to
continue to live now? Do I have the strength to carry
on for even one more day?

Tragedy can bring out our authentic concern for
one another. Reaching out and accepting care and
comfort can see us through times that would otherwise
be unbearable.

Living through a tragic event unmasks us, strips
us of pretense. This is who we are, this is what we
have. It can get us in touch with our deepest selves and
regenerate our humanity. Tragedy links us one to
another, if we let it.

We can trust that our life experience has prepared
us to survive. Tragedy can teach us what nothing else
can. We may not believe it now, but soon enough we'll
be grateful for what it had to teach, for the opportunity
it gave us to reach out and receive.

Today, let me trust in the wisdom of tragedy.

*In the middle of life's road, I found myself in
a dark woods. The straight way ahead lost.*

Dante Alighieri

Dante was in his forties and in exile from Florence when he began the Divine Comedy, his greatest work. It was his vision of a journey through Hell, Purgatory, and Paradise. Dante had crossed the frontier between growing up and growing old.

Loneliness seems to mark the frontier of all midlife crises and second journeys. Deep inertia and feelings of being lost and alone may torment us. These same feelings, however, because they reach so deep, stir old creative juices. Perhaps a sudden event propels us out of our isolation. Having tasted renewal, most of us will do almost anything to hold on to it. We may be asking, who is the real me? How do I want to live the rest of my life? And we scramble to find the answers out there, where we've been taught to look.

To answer these questions, however, we need to return to the well we rediscovered at our lowest ebb. That descent is perhaps exactly what we needed to cross this latest frontier. Without it, we would still be looking for the answers out there, rather than within, where they have always been.

*Today, let me embrace the difficult question I have yet
to answer about myself.*

If a word spoken in its time is worth one piece of money, silence in its time is worth two.

The Talmud

Learning when to keep our mouths shut and be quiet is an art. Silence can be a gift we give to others when they are hurting. When our loved ones make mistakes, do we need to rub salt in their wounds?

We are our own worst critics, and oversensitive to shortcomings. What our friends might need more than anything is a hug, or a silent, accepting smile.

When they goof up, sometimes we feel compelled to put our two cents in. We may feel some old need to make this failure a good lesson for the other person. Do we have an exaggerated sense of our own purpose and power in those moments? Our "judge's bench" is a lonely spot that places us above others.

Time teaches us the dignity that only silence can confer. It is a gift from our heart that others will bless us for.

Today, let me think about how I would like to be treated before I respond to someone who has made a mistake.

July 12

When you see a man in distress, recognize him as a fellow man.

Seneca

Depression is like taking a lonely walk down a long corridor, and the door at the very end is death. Those of us who have approached that last door need to be reminded that all along the corridor to the right and left are other doors. These other doors are ways out of pain.

From inside the dark place that is depression, it can look like there is no way out, no relief from pain. From outside that room, we know this isn't true, that there are alternatives. But depression speaks in absolutes, not alternatives. It is an illness.

If we are depressed or know someone who is, we must take it seriously. We can reach out, for help, or to help. No one needs to walk that hall alone.

We are never responsible for another's pain, but we can make a difference in their lives just as they make a difference in ours. No gift is too small, especially the gift of hope.

Today, give me the courage to reach out, for myself or for my depressed friend.

. . . with an eye made quiet by the power of harmony, and the deep power of joy, we see into the life of things.

William Wordsworth

Balance and harmony are the guardian angels of decisions. As we grow to cherish peace and order in our lives, we become committed to protecting our serenity.

Decisions become simpler to make when we learn to listen to our internal messages. By tuning in to what we really think and feel about a decision, we can come to know the sound and feel of right and wrong. When we're on the right track, the forests of confusion seem to open up; we experience a sense of "Ah, yes! That's right for me." When we try to force an unhealthy choice, we get lost in the woods and our path seems confused and dark. Somehow we've known all along this wasn't the right way. We could feel it. But we were egged on by fear or denial or pressure from another.

There are no perfect decisions. Life is never that clean. All of us at one time or another regret a choice we've made. But as we rely more on our felt sense of right and wrong and less on what others would have us choose, our decisions will always be right, no matter what the outcome.

Today, let me think less and feel more about the decisions I make.

> *It is likely that we experience the Father's*
> *forgiveness of us more when we in turn*
> *forgive our fellow human beings.*
>
> *Marvin Gawryn*

Mid-life is the time to examine old grudges, to take another look at the people who hurt us a long time ago. Maybe we had something to do with what happened. Maybe not. But if we're still feeling hate or resentment, the pain is as alive as if it just happened this morning.

The act of forgiving can be ennobling and humbling and healing. Whenever we forgive another we are in fact forgiving ourselves—for harsh judgment, arrogance, superiority, insecurity. We are acknowledging both the weakness and the strength of the person we forgive, as well as ourselves.

The paradox is that we receive forgiveness as we forgive, although that may be far from our original intention. Old fears and rigid views are dissolved, and we can get on with our lives unshackled by the past. Forgiveness can finally close that old wound. It can free us to love others whole.

Today, let me forgive my enemy. Let me realize we are both imperfect, fallible people.

I do not expect anything from others so their actions cannot be in opposition to wishes of mine.

Swami Sri Yukteswar

Our need to control other people, places, and things is like a poisonous snake that can turn back and attack us. Managing the lives of our family, friends, and co-workers is a thankless job that leads to frustration and anger. We get angry when people don't do things our way and they get angry because they resent being told what to do.

It is possible to become so involved in judging and directing the lives of others that we lose our own lives. How do we tell if we are overly involved and too controlling? A good way to measure our take-charge behavior is to get honest on paper about all the things we worry about, all the advice we give, all the ways we try to control others, and how we feel if people don't do things our way. Sharing our list with an objective party is a beginning in sorting out our controlling behavior.

As we learn to let go of others, we can get back our own lives unhampered by everyone else's problems.

Today, help me get honest about how I judge and try to control others.

*Two myths must be shattered: that of the
evil stepparent and the myth of instant love,
which places unrealistic demands on all
members of the blended family.*

       Claire Berman

When we first open our homes to stepchildren we
are keenly aware that they are a part of the package we
did not bargain for. Like them or not, we did not
choose them.

Children bond instinctively with the parents or
guardians with whom they share their earliest years.
In any struggle they are likely to side against us. The
challenge then is for us to remain as patient and
accepting as possible. Time can smooth this initially
rough dynamic.

Our stepchildren may become major channels for
our growth; we in turn may be the instruments
through which they have a real chance for a healthy
life. Let us never minimize our potential for influence.

In time, a respect and caring may emerge, not out
of obligation; it simply happens. We may find ourselves applauding their individuality, so different from
ours. And we may find them appreciating us, and the
emotional support we've given.

*Today, let me be patient with myself and my step-
children and allow time to draw us into the right
relationship.*

You don't choose your family. They are
God's gift to you, as you are to them.

Desmond Tutu

No sooner are our children out of our nest and off on their own when caring for our parents becomes an issue. Ties of blood and obligation can engulf us rapidly. We feel responsible for them much as we did toward our children.

For many of us, it's all too easy to put our needs on the back burner and become the dutiful daughter or son once again. Better that, we may think, than the conflicts that would ensue should we assert ourselves. Better that then face our parents as the adults we are rather than the children they may still perceive us to be. So, many of us keep the peace. But it's our loss.

By being models of self-denial we hurt our children and ourselves. We pass up what may be the only chance to know our parents, adult to adult, conflicts and all.

Little by little, if it's safe, we might let ourselves be known to them. This may encourage them to do likewise. To know them may mean ultimately to know ourselves. Thus are we truly gifts to each other.

Today, let me risk being myself with my parents.

July 18

Whatever mark I leave behind will be my sunset, and those who might observe it some day will hold me accountable for the feel of its light.

Gordon Parks

We each bring a gift to life that we will leave behind, whether it's just our smile or a symphony. This is our legacy. The gifts that will be our legacy come from the part of us that wishes ardently to live and feels vitally alive. We can find our gifts in whatever makes us feel this way: our work, our relationships, our connection to the land, the community, the larger world. We can find them in our voices, in our handwriting, in our skill with a hammer or a kitchen knife.

Our gifts are always with us. Others can see them when we cannot. It is easy to lose sight of them when we compare ourselves to others. Or when we are busy. To see them we must slow down and listen. When we can't find them we have only to wait for the next time we feel happy. Our gifts are very close to the surface then. They are the hands of our spirit, able to reach—and to bless and heal—where our bodies cannot.

Today, let me trust that I have a legacy to offer life.

I'm always on vacation.

   Mahatma Gandhi

In his late seventies, Gandhi worked fifteen hours a day, seven days a week without tension and fatigue, because he was able to drop his work at will. He had developed remarkable powers of concentration that allowed him to focus completely on the matter at hand. His resources were not depleted by a cluttered mind full of unfinished business and yesterday's troubles.

When asked by a western journalist how he could work like this for fifty years without a vacation, Gandhi replied, "I'm always on vacation."

When work is part play and meditation, it can refresh rather than deplete us. Although we may not yet have a lot of choice about the work we do, we can change our approach to it. We can focus on the aspects we do like, however small, however invisible those aspects may be to others.

When we play and meditate we speak in silence, listen in silence, ask for a silent mind. We can do likewise when we work. When we are one with whatever we're doing, we have no need to be anywhere but where we are.

Today, let me learn how to unclutter my mind and focus on whatever I am doing.

*If I had two loaves of bread, I would sell
one and buy hyacinths for they would feed
my soul.*

The Koran

The hardest hunger to bear is that of our souls. When our spirit is nourished our hearts and bodies sing; joy is no stranger. Our spiritual development asks that we say yes to the people, places, and things in our lives that nurture us. It asks, too, that we say no to those things that don't.

Lives cluttered with meetings, telephone calls, appointments, and endless lists of things to do leave little room inside us for the soul's flowers to grow. To make that room we must review our priorities. They most likely have changed since we first established our schedules. Where and how can we cut back?

That first meeting we bow out of may be a rough one. We may feel guilt. We may not be used to putting ourselves first. People may be disappointed or angry with us.

It's a choice. One that at first may not feel so good. We can trust, however, that the very sense that tells us what to cut out of our lives can in time tell us what to fill them in with.

Today, let me get honest about my life. Do I give myself the time to grow spiritually?

Most importantly, be prepared to be happy.
The women who say they dread widowhood
are a royal pain in the butt.

Kent Collins

There is nothing to be said about losing a spouse, or fearing the loss. When it happens we grieve. We can do ourselves a great kindness if we surrender to the wisdom of grief, to its stages as they unfold.

Grief has its own rhythms. They are one with us. They issue from the part of us that would have us live and thrive no matter what happens to us, no matter who or what we lose.

It can be difficult, if not impossible, to believe we could even be happy again, but we will. There is yet another self inside us waiting to be born, waiting for grief to give birth to him or her. We are strangers yet to this new self, but ardent self-care and reaching for help can ease the labor. In the death of our spouse is ultimately our new life.

Today, let me believe in the necessity of my life going on, no matter what my losses.

July 22

We must combine the toughness of the ser-
pent and the softness of the dove, a tough
mind and tender heart.

Martin Luther King, Jr.

What will we do about our old enemies? Are there people in our lives unworthy of our forgiveness? Have they really wounded us beyond repair? Is holding a grudge still necessary?

To forgive or not to forgive is a serious decision that requires careful thought. Perhaps it is time to take our old resentments out of the closet and decide if we still want them taking up space in our wardrobe of life. Resentments can be like old clothes we hate to part with. What if we need them again? Is it safe to part with them? Will there ever be a right time to let go? Can we trust that time has made us tough enough to risk having a tender heart? How would it be to our advantage to forgive our enemies?

Forgiveness can set us free. When we forgive we are no longer attached. We give up what may have become a monstrous weight.

Forgiveness cannot be forced, but it can be coaxed forth. If we provide a safe arena for all our feelings about the person, forgiveness will likely be among them.

Today, let me trust my ability to forgive and survive.

*I got to the point where material things
don't mean a darn thing to me anymore.
I feel good about that.*

Tom Monaghan

For many of us our adult years have been taken up
with the quest for success as we have understood it:
houses, cars, salary, position, academic degrees. Now,
however, we may be questioning the very values that
have led us to acquire these things. Maybe we are asking ourselves, "Is this the 'good life'? What's the
point?"

Many of us are turning inward. This doesn't
mean we need to reject material success, only that we
need to reframe it. We need to put things in their
place.

We don't have to give things away—though we
can if we want—or repudiate our creature comforts.
Imposed self-denial will only dig us in deeper. What
we can do is re-evaluate what we have—our jobs
and our possessions—in the light of our spiritual
aspirations.

If we, as spiritual beings, are coming to value
honesty, wholeness, balance, silence, integrity, community, we can inject them into what we do and what
we have. To become spiritual we need not start from
scratch. We can take what we already have and make
it whole.

*Today, help me see the things around me for what
they are.*

July 24

The theme song for the chronically bored is called: "I am unhappy. What are you going to do about it?"

Edward H. Scissons

Do we blame someone else when we're restless or bored? Do we expect that they can or should make us feel better, or at least distract us from ourselves? Do we go to them with this expectation?

If we do, it isn't fair to them or us. We all lapse now and then when it comes to taking responsibility for our feelings. It's especially easy to do so when we're bored. We don't exactly feel bad, but we don't feel good either. We may not know what we need or want. Maybe we feel crabby. Maybe the little kid in us is tired of working so hard and wants someone else to just know this without our telling them. And maybe, too, we want them to know what we want and need.

The haze of boredom is often a cover for anger or pain, or some other strong feeling. If we can face the feeling and safely release it—and we can, by talking or moving or crying or beating a pillow—we'll probably find our boredom released with it. Or at least we'll have an idea about what we want or need. Then we can set about getting it without expecting someone else to do it for us.

Today, help me know when boredom is a cover for some other feeling. Help me safely release it.

Don't hurry, don't worry, don't compare.
> *Roger Stanz*

Are we slaves to the clock or the calendar? Are we running too late, too early, too lengthy? Do we hurry to meet deadlines, set dates rigidly, organize ourselves too tightly? Being compulsive about time can hurt us. It can keep us from listening to ourselves and learning our own rhythms.

Today, certain African tribal peoples still live by nature's clock. They know neither the day nor year of their birth, and they have no concept of months. They don't need to. They live by the sun and the seasons and pace themselves accordingly.

In the spiritual realm everything unfolds as it should. We are never late; we never miss anything intended for us. We accomplish what we are meant to do in spite of ourselves.

We can loosen the reins on time and not come undone. We can trust that whatever we seek will unfold, not on our timetable, but on God's. We can rest with this knowledge. We don't have to push so hard.

Today, let me allow this day to shape itself as though I were not controlling it.

> *There is a great mystery and powerful*
> *music playing that we don't hear and sto-*
> *ries full of magic, so many stories that life*
> *isn't long enough to tell them all.*
>
> *Garrison Keillor*

The treasures of our world are endless. In one lifetime we can only begin to scratch the surface of life's
beauties. Art, music, travel, ancient mysteries, reading, writing, friendship, love, nature's seasons, wild
animals, goldfish—all are life's treasures. Time spent
doing nothing and time spent thinking, running,
walking, swimming, jogging, and juggling are also
today's gifts to us. The world is our treasure chest and
we have the key.

Each day we get to choose how we will see the
world. Do we choose light-colored glasses or dark? If
light, we are choosing to avail ourselves of the possibilities and pleasures each moment of living has to
offer. When we choose light-colored glasses we are
open to awe and wonder. We deepen and widen our
field of vision to see what is already there. We see miracles in everyday things. We have only to open our
eyes and ears.

Today, let me relish and cherish the gifts that are mine
for the asking.

*A man travels the world over in search of
what he needs and returns home to find it.*

George Moore

When we feel alienated or defeated, or feel a sense
of futility about our current state, we may yearn to find
a place of comfort. We may feel an overwhelming
need to go home to a place where care and unconditional love abound.

Does such a place exist? By now we may have created many homes for ourselves, yet once again restlessness and discontent engulf us.

While we may in fact yearn for a physical place, a
true home, we may never find it until we find it within
ourselves, with the god of our understanding. No
place and no person can be home if we are not at home
within ourselves.

This journey home can be routed by none but ourselves. It can take everything in us to refuse to listen to
those who would tell us who our god is, where our true
home is, where in fact we belong. But this is the challenge: to listen to ourselves, to the one who knows. We
are the only ones who can take us to our god, who then
can take us home.

*Today, let me experience for a few moments that spiri-
tual peace I need.*

You have to give it all you have, especially since you never know how long the good times will last.

Lee Iacocca

For many of us, saying "I love you" is awkward and difficult. Maybe our actions express what we cannot say. Are we willing to stand by the ones we love? Do we let them know how important our relationship is? Do we share our thoughts and feelings? Are we willing to go out of our way for them? Are we faithful to them? Do we refrain from blaming, alibis, indifference, and dishonesty?

If we can answer yes to these questions, we have a loving relationship. But does our partner know it? Learning to say I love you can insure that they do. We may at first feel awkward and self-conscious, but with practice the awkwardness will dissolve. Our relationships will be the stronger for it.

Today, let me feast myself and my partner with a spontaneous gesture or word to express my love.

*What hours, O what black hours we have
spent this night.*

Gerard Manley Hopkins

It is difficult to be told that the death of a loved one is a "normal" life crisis. But unlike marriage, parenthood, job-changing or divorce, we feel we have fewer guides to lead us through this agonizing process.

If we allow ourselves to experience our pain as it unfolds, we can prevent the deeper pain of delayed or distorted grief, which can cripple us unnecessarily for too many years.

It is also essential to our health that we release our feelings. We are right to cry openly, right to feel sad, angry, helpless, and abandoned in our grief. This is natural. Serious illness can result if we repress or deny the emotional impact of the loss of a loved one too long.

Even though we feel terrible in mind and body, it is right for us to feel that way as we proceed through the stages of grief. It is a very slow process, but it does end in time and the sun will shine on us again.

Today, let me continue to grieve so that eventually I might focus my energies toward a good future for myself.

> *To forgive is to give . . . to give some actual definite good in return for evil given.*
>
> H. Emilie Cady

Among certain Native American tribes it once was customary to return right for wrong. When a man was wronged, he would tie his best pony outside the wrongdoer's teepee as a gesture of forgiveness and peace.

For many of us this type of forgiveness might seem ridiculous not to mention self-destructive and confusing. It is, if we are feeling pressured to forgive before we're ready, before we've expressed our anger about the wrong. Forgiveness, when forced, is not forgiveness. Like grief, it has its own rhythms that must be honored.

If, however, we are stuck in resentment, if anger has become a ball and chain, forgiveness can free us. An attitude of forgiveness, which looks for the good behind the behavior that is bad, can disarm the enemy. It can open us to feelings about the other we may not have been willing to consider. It can give us peace. We may find that when one party resigns from the battle, the war ends.

Today, let me be willing to step back and think through my reactions in a conflict.

We are not going to be able to control the destiny of our children. Only God's shoulders are big enough for this job.

Sam Friend

No matter how much we worry and try to protect our children from an unsafe world, we eventually learn that we are not in charge. Worry does not have magical powers of protection; it cannot keep those we love safe.

In 1911 a man went over Niagara Falls in a barrel and survived. The story says he broke many bones but recovered sufficiently to embark on a worldwide lecture tour. In New Zealand he slipped on a banana peel and died. So much for who's in charge.

It can be a great relief to finally understand that we can care for our children, but ultimately we are not responsible for them. Worry is no measure of love. Neither is protection that shields them from their pain. We need to ask ourselves, who are we really doing this for? Who are we if we are not worried?

We can learn to worry less, to turn our worries over to God. When we are not worrying about our children we have more room to attend to our own lives. We have more room to attend to the real concerns our children bring us, the things we can do something about.

Today, help me know that I can't protect my children from life's banana peels.

August 1

*A mature spiritual man will make sure that
his words are positive and creative.*
Dr. Paul Yonggi Cho

Yonggi Cho thinks most people walk around believing they are "accidents waiting to happen." He disagrees. So would God. We are never accidents. We live our lives according to God's plan, and in this plan there are no accidents. On days when it's hard to get out of bed, when our moods seem like endless rainy days, it may be hard to think so. Maybe on these days we need to connect with someone who can affirm our goodness and our gifts. Someone who can see the beauty in us when we cannot see it for ourselves. Someone who can help revive our hope.

Attitude change can happen in an instant with the smallest bit of encouragement. That little bit of encouragement can get us across the one threshold we believed we could not cross, and so change our day. It can poke holes in our belief about being an accident. Encouragement then, when sincere, can be the greatest of gifts, to give or receive.

Today, let me choose to get out of bed on the right side, ready to enter my day with positive energy.

We may put so much negative energy into resisting our goal that we have little energy left over to do the necessary work.

Elmer Wilkenson

We all seem to have a particular problem that won't budge, no matter what we try. Maybe it's resistance to starting an exercise program, losing twenty pounds, being kind to our mother-in-law, going back to school, or developing a hobby. No matter what angle we approach it from, nothing seems to work. Paralysis may set in. We can't stop feeling bad about it.

If we really want to accomplish this goal, today challenges us to find the first step, however small, in that direction. There may never be the exact right time to begin anything we've been resisting, so with the help of our Higher Power we can ask to begin today. Perhaps the first step is our willingness to begin or the plan itself. Whatever it is, we need to honor our energy level and pace ourselves accordingly. We are doing this for, not to ourselves.

Small steps are an antidote for discouragement and giving up on goals. Our Higher Power helps us as we put one foot in front of the other. Small steps can become fulfilled dreams.

Today, let me realize that I don't always have to like the process of reaching my goal. Help me trust enough to do it anyway.

August 3

Adventure is the champagne of life.
        G.K. Chesterton

If we hear ourselves chronically complaining, if we're feeling bored or listless, chances are we've been backing away from life. We may have become, without realizing it, more the spectator than the actor.

Boldness can be scary. Yet so many rewards result from taking action. To take a risk, no matter how small, is to be open to adventure.

When we say or do the unexpected without worrying about how messy, incoherent, or disorderly we are, we may feel a stirring inside. It's adrenaline, our life reasserting itself. Whatever we do, it need not be irresponsible or self-destructive. The smallest things, if they are risky for us, can be all we need to get out from under what may at times feel like an oppressive weight of responsibility.

Then, having thrown caution to the wind, we can return to our lives renewed and recommitted. We will want to be there.

Today, let me pray for the courage to change the things I can.

Wisdom is to finish the moment, to find the journey's end in every step of the road.
        Ralph Waldo Emerson

What would it be like if we were truly present—enough so that we really could finish the moment, here and now? Usually we find ourselves a few steps behind or ahead of our lives. Our internal clocks are often set ten minutes fast. Let's get there before the next guy! If I get this work done faster, I'll be able to start my new project sooner. Hurry, Hurry, Stop!

"Make Today Count" is a support group for cancer patients. Participants find that the quality of life lived in the moment is always the richest and most healing.

How can we make all our days count if we're living with one foot in yesterday and the other foot in tomorrow? This moment is all that truly belongs to us. Yesterday is a memory and tomorrow a dream. But we can make today count.

Today, let me try not to get too far ahead of myself.

August 5

In the true man there is a child concealed—
who wants to play.

Friedrich Nietzsche

Watching young children leap and romp and frolic can evoke nostalgia. We sigh and lumber on, for we believe adults should not play. We're aware of the need for leisure and recreation, but we see them as stress-reducers; they balance our tendency to over-work. We see sports as an outlet for aggression and competitiveness.

Have we become so serious that we've lost our capacity for play as simply pleasure? What do we do for sheer enjoyment, with movement and looseness, just for the fun of it?

Unstructured, frivolous play taps the spontaneous child within us, the child who would be creative if only we would let him or her out to play. Play shakes loose aspects of ourselves we may have thought were dead but have only been dormant. Play lets the silly, outrageous child within us renew the serious adult. When we play we feel deeply, without a doubt, how good it is to be alive.

Today, when no one is looking, let me express myself playfully, just for the fun of it.

*The world is charged with the grandeur
of God.*

Gerard Manley Hopkins

Today we can receive the healing power of nature.
We can hear the wind and rain in the trees. We can
observe the gentleness with which a cardinal feeds its
mate. We can remember the smell of the first daffodil
in April or the wide orange light of the harvest moon
rising in the east.

Maybe we know the absolute silence of the high
desert in the southwest or how a wheat field in Kansas
looks at dawn, the mist that hangs over it in pockets.
Or the shafts of light that turn a forest into a cathedral.

Even if we are city- or house-bound we can still
receive from nature. One flower or houseplant can do
it. Or stepping outside for air. Or closing our eyes and
breathing with the wind. No grand vistas are required.
Nature gives and asks nothing in return, only that
we see.

*Today, let me soak up nature's beauty, color, and
sound. It is God's daily tranquilizer prescribed just
for me.*

August 7

*Inside the tough-talking, hard jogging man
of forty who is identified largely by his
work, there is a boy trying not to cry,
"Time's running out."*

Gail Sheehy

Mid-life catches many of us unaware. Women
have been watching their bodies change since they
were teens, but in a culture that exalts youth, signs of
aging can be traumatic. Women, too, have the loss of
their role as mother to deal with as their children
leave. Men may be little prepared for the physical
changes that just seem to happen to their mid-life
bodies. Suddenly they may realize that there are some
things no amount of power, effort, or determination
can alter. We have run companies and households, but
we are powerless to stop the changes in our bodies and
emotions.

Many of us may now be faced with questions we
have no answers to. Who am I really, without my old
familiar role? What's left for me now to dream about?
What will happen to me?

We need to be patient with our questions and ourselves. Mid-life means struggle and re-evaluation. It is
not an easy transition. Pretending not to feel the pain
of going through it hurts us worse and confuses those
close to us. Mid-life challenges us not to deny it, but to
identify and begin to talk about our changing feelings
and awareness. The more we talk, the better we will
feel. And we'll find out we're not alone.

*Today, help me see my changing self as a necessary
bridge to a richer life.*

*If a marriage fails, it's always both people's
responsibility. Part of getting better is for
both to realize the responsibility they have
for the failure.*

Jane Fonda

Acknowledging that a relationship has in fact
ended and taking responsibility for our part in its
downfall may take years, especially if the ending was
sudden or we were the ones who were left. Only we
and our partners know the inner workings of our marriage. So only we know why it ended. And only we
can get at the truth it takes to heal.

To heal from a broken relationship, as from any
trauma, we must first honestly face what happened.
We must surrender to the impact, let ourselves feel the
pain without denying or minimizing it. This loss is like
a death. We have much to grieve. Our grief has its own
rhythm and its own timetable. To challenge either is to
hurt ourselves. Because we have what it takes to be
honest with ourselves, we have what it takes to be gentle with ourselves, to forgive ourselves in our grief.
This process can be trusted.

*Today, let me continue confidently with daily living,
while I slowly, gently attend to the layers of my grief.*

August 9

Forgiveness is a thought, not a behavior. It is an inner expression of self-respect and integrity. The grounds for forgiving are simple: grievances are unworthy of you.

Hugh Prather

No one avoids being hurt by life. Those we love the most have the ability to hurt us the most deeply. Some of us seem to make a hobby of collecting and reliving grievances. We are keenly sensitive to oversights, neglect, and hurts. Our nervous systems seem to be radar-equipped to detect and point out the failings of others. We often carry a full sack of resentment on our shoulders each day.

Gradually, we get stooped and weighed down by not forgiving others. The energy it takes to carry a grievance robs us of our natural lightness and gentleness.

Forgiveness asks that we change our attitude about living. It asks that we acknowledge our need for peace by forgiving, thus letting go of the power we give others to hurt us.

Today, let me carry a candle of peace to everyone I meet.

Go where your best prayers take you.
Frederick Buechner

The higher choice is the best choice, but often the most difficult. It is getting out of bed on a cold morning a half hour earlier to exercise or have quiet time. It is being committed to caring for ourselves and others in the best way we can. It is promptly saying "I'm sorry" when we've wronged someone. It is saying goodbye to a relationship that keeps us in painful stagnation and conflict. It is sometimes being cheerful when we don't feel we can, in hopes that by doing so our day will get better.

The higher choice is forgiving ourselves for all the moments when we haven't been willing to make the higher choice. Perhaps self-compassion is actually the highest choice of all.

Today, let me love myself enough to be willing to make decisions that are in my healthiest interest.

August 11

*To live in our society, which encourages us
to walk two by two, takes the courage of
convictions when you are single and walk
alone for whatever reason.*

Susan Deitz

Singleness should never be interpreted as a mandate to go it alone. Stoicism and isolation are not components of a successful single life. We don't have to belittle our desire for help. We all need others for support and information so it just makes plain good sense to take advantage of every shred of expertise available through reading, friends, and work.

We all need feedback—someone to bounce ideas around with, someone who is honest enough to give us a straight answer. Having people we can count on (and who, in turn, can count on us) is essential for us. It is an act of self-love. Knowing others who care about us are out there, whether or not we ever use them, weakens the hold fear or pride may have on us.

We don't have to handle everything alone. There is nothing we need to prove. Rather, recognizing when we need help is a sign of growth and health.

*Today, let me reach out to others when my problems
seem larger than life.*

*Never change a winning game; always
change a losing one.*

       Bill Tilden

Some of us have lived in abusive relationships for
so many years that we dare not label them as such.
Abuse is force in any form, not only the physical. If we
are threatened or constantly criticized, if we are
coerced into doing anything we don't want to do, we
are being abused. If we are being manipulated, we are
being abused. The range is wide. When someone
degrades us, refuses to address our needs, or tries to
control what we do, say, or think, we are being abused.

None of this is normal. No one deserves this. No
human being needs to tolerate it. There are ways out.

The first step is seeing the abuse for what it is.
The next is telling someone we trust. Then we must
get angry with our abuser, although we need not confront him or her. If we don't turn our anger outward,
where it belongs, we may continue to turn it inward,
against ourselves, or vent it onto someone who doesn't
deserve it.

There are so many survivors. When we break our
silence we can discover them. With their help we can
heal.

*Today, let me know abuse when I see it, and help me
tell someone about it.*

August 13

Are the names of the new music groups on the radio as familiar to you as the atomic weight of lead? A survey says you're middle-aged if you can't peg those music groups.

Karen Peterson

Keeping up with youthful preoccupations—fads, slang, music, clothes—can be wearying. Do we really want to immerse ourselves in it? Are we trying to prove something?

Our culture would have us identify with the things of youth. To do so completely, however, is to deny a central truth—that how old we are has everything to do with who we are. When we deny what we've been taught to call the curses of age, it's too easy to deny all the growth and the good.

There are those people who exalt in their age. We can learn from them. We can rethink what it means to grow old. Youth need not be a foreign country to us, but an obsession with its ways, things, and images can harm us. Age is rich. We can be rich with age.

Today, let me turn down their music so I can hear and enjoy my own.

*With my friend I may share my asocial,
heretical, treasonous, anti-social, tabooed
or outrageous ideas, visions and feelings.*

       Sam Keen

What a relief to sit down with good friends and feel the freedom to pour out our hearts. We don't have to censor or edit ourselves. We don't have to agree with them, please them, or pretend to be feeling something we're not. With good friends we can rest. We can take great comfort in the knowledge that they are on our side even when we find it difficult to see merit in ourselves.

With real friends we are transformed. We can help each other heal. The unconditional love that is the center of real friendship can enable us, finally, to talk about the things we're most ashamed of. To entrust our secrets to another is the beginning of healing. This great gift of friendship can see us through anything. It is worth every effort at cultivation.

Today, let me tell my friends how happy I am to have them in my life.

August 15

Victory is given to the one who dares to be alone.

Anthony de Mello

Learning the pleasures of solitude is a great victory. Finding comfort and peace in our own company is restorative. If we give ourselves enough time and space, solitude can give us what no person can. Alone, we can find out what we are thinking about. Away from others who may never tire of telling us what is good for us, we may find out from the ultimate authority—ourselves. We can discover what is essential to us, what we can and cannot live with.

Solitude is different from isolation. In solitude we find renewal and so return to others strengthened. In isolation, we withdraw into ourselves to avoid others. Isolation separates us from our real selves and others; solitude makes a feast of our humanness and goodness so we might share it with others when we return to the table of life.

Today, let me risk getting to know my self better and face my fear of spending quiet time alone.

The mother must not only tolerate she must wish and support the child's separation.
Erich Fromm

Loving our children means being able to say goodbye. It means letting go of any expectation that they will or can or should fill our needs. It means recognizing their right to their own lives played by their own rules. When we acknowledge and express our grief and resistance and come to support our children's separation, we give them the gift of their own lives.

As young adults, our children are leading lives defined by their values. We may not like their lifestyle, but we are utterly powerless to change them. We may pressure them into compliance, but sooner or later they will rebel and return to their own lives. The best way not to meddle in our children's lives is to put energy back into our own.

Rediscovering ourselves as men and women instead of as Mom and Dad can renew us. Perhaps we have cared for our children and neglected ourselves. Perhaps we think about what we can accomplish for them rather than what we can accomplish for us, how we can control their lives rather than our own. Picking up where we left off with ourselves isn't easy, but it is the best gift we can give our children and ourselves.

Today, let me let go of my children. Help me remember that the only answers I have are for my own life.

Freedom is the open window through which pours the dignity of the human spirit.

Herbert Hoover

When we give up our freedom to choose, or when we don't feel free to follow our inner voice, we die a little inside. Maturity teaches us to be open to learning from others, but we still have the right to make mistakes and the right to learn from our mistakes. The final word remains our own.

Nothing will stifle and drown a relationship quicker than when one adult does not respect the other's right to decide. Some decisions are negotiable, and good partnerships contain a "win-win" clause in which each person has a voice. But some decisions are a matter of individual conscience and we have no right to interfere with that process. Do our partners encourage us to reach our own conclusions and decide for ourselves? Do we respect our partner's right to do likewise? Are there subtle or not so subtle ways in which we try to curtail the other's freedom?

Relationships thrive when each gives the other the freedom to decide. When we give someone wings, we give them the freedom to fly with us.

Today, let me give my partner the freedom to follow the dictates of his or her own conscience.

> *Before I built a wall I'd ask to know what I
> was walling in or walling out.*
>
> *Robert Frost*

Walls can protect us but they can also isolate us.
There are times when it is in our best interest to detach
from someone we love. Whether they are hurting us or
themselves, the best thing we can do is build a wall.
We can learn, for example, to stop rescuing and shield-
ing our children from the consequences of their behaviors. Building such a wall says, "I am here for you, but
there are limits on what I will do for you."

Sometimes building walls is the only way to
change. Walling off certain people or walling ourselves in may not feel so good at first. We may meet
with fierce resistance. It looks very much out of character to those who want in. But we can trust our
instincts on this, and know that we have a choice. No
wall need be permanent. No wall need be built without a door. Walls, for a time, can be just the thing we
need in order to heal.

*Today, let me trust the walls I build. Help me see when
and where to build them and to break them down.*

All we need is to imagine our ability to love developing until it embraces the totality of men and of the earth.

Pierre Teilhard de Chardin

Fairy tales, soap operas, and romantic songs have given love a bad name. They've taught us that love is vested in only one person and that love is a destination to be discovered at any cost. Then in our search for the perfect lover, we no doubt find a very real human being, possessed of no miracle solutions for happiness.

Love will continue to disappoint us unless we are willing to cultivate a wider vision. Perhaps love is part of our answer instead of our only answer. Developing a wider vision enables us to experience love as a journey instead of a destination and as a process instead of a solution.

Today we can reach out to others with a loving hand and a smile rather than waiting for someone to give to us. Love brings us great joy, great rewards when we allow it to flow from our own heart out to others. The more we enjoy life and take the time to reach out to others, the more love we give, and the more loved we will feel.

Today, let me trust that my capacity for loving is abundant.

Sometimes I actually ache in my need to be held by another human being.

John Williams

The feeling of longing that can accompany alone-ness is difficult to describe. It is a seemingly bottom-less yearning, feeling rebuffed again and again by the raw fact of there being no one there to touch and hold on to. It is our healthy need to share, connect with, and love another human being. This longing goes deeper than sexuality, deeper than skin hunger. It is our spirit crying to be known by another.

A widow who had lived alone for many years said the only way she could live with the empty place in her heart was one day at a time. In confronting the loneli-ness of a solitary life we confront ourselves. We can learn the value of loving that in the past we may have taken for granted. We can learn that no one person can fill that hole, assuage that ache. Only we can, with God's help.

A nurturing relationship is a gift, not a guarantee. Even without one, we are still whole. We can still con-nect. We can still fill the longing. There's more than one person and one way.

Today, let me embrace my loneliness yet continue to reach out to others.

August 21

Is there no pity sitting in the clouds,
That sees into the bottom of my grief?

William Shakespeare

Divorce is a shattering experience. The end of a marriage, the end of so much that is so familiar we don't even see it, can turn our lives upside down. Even when we know it is in our best interest, divorce can still be devastating.

Grief takes many forms. People in painful marriages often grieve for years before they actually divorce. When our partner wants to end our marriage and we don't, there is another kind of grief, full of rage, shame, and powerlessness. Accepting what we don't want takes enormous faith and time, but can only happen once we've expressed the rage, the shame, the powerlessness—whatever feelings we have about what has happened to us. Where rage leaves, serenity can enter. In fits and starts we rebuild from the ground up, but stronger.

Maybe we feel used up, like we have nothing left to give or there's nobody home to receive. But remarkably, even this passes. Threaded through our season of grief and pain are peace and hope. At the end—and it does end—lies choice.

Today, let me take care of myself. Help me trust that God's will for me is perfect.

*Nature's peace will flow into you as the sun
shines into the trees. The winds will blow
their freshness into you, and the storms
their energy, while cares will drop off like
autumn leaves.*

    John Muir

Walking is excellent physical, spiritual, and emotional therapy. One counselor is so thoroughly convinced of its power to heal that she won't counsel anyone unless they walk 20 minutes each day.

Whether in our cars or homes or offices, most of us live lives that happen inside, often behind windows that don't open. Walking reconnects us to the world and to the life of the senses.

We remember we are bodies. We remember our breath. We can take comfort from the continuity of nature or the street. Living inside makes it all too easy to live inside our heads. Our senses, invigorated by weather, by air and sky and color and sound, are a bridge to the larger world. Thus connected, we gain perspective on ourselves.

Walking is a physical tonic, an antidote to worry and mild depression, a meditation. Literally putting one foot in front of the other can change the course of our days.

Today, let me take a walk.

*No one is with me. No one keeps me safe.
There is no one who won't ever leave me
alone.*

> *Gail Sheehy*

In the decade between 35 and 45 we encounter many of the major issues of mid-life, not the least of which is our aloneness. By now we've won and lost enough to be familiar with the solitude that lies behind the crest of each victory or failure. Whether we share our bed with someone or not, we sleep alone. We take our own measure in the moments before sleep.

When we were children afraid of the dark, we needed to believe we'd never be alone. We still may harbor the hope that someone will always be there to keep us safe from monsters. Until we realize that we are safe in our own solitude, the battle between adult and child will rage. Until we embrace the solitary part of ourselves, we will continue to expect others to fill our emptiness and rage at them when they don't.

Embracing solitude and learning to rejoice in our own company is the dessert of life. When we become comfortable sitting still with ourselves, we learn we have little to fear. When we step across the threshold into our own life and good company we meet our resources. Life may not protect us from monsters but it gives us the resources to deal with them.

Today, let me not fear the journey into knowing myself. Teach me to look for safety and answers within.

*Knowledge is received only in those
moments in which every judgment, every
criticism coming from ourselves is silent.*

Rudolf Steiner

It's hard to learn about ourselves when our internal critic is sitting perched on our shoulder ready to attack. When this is happening nothing looks good. We see the world and ourselves through a dusty, distorted lens. Persistent self-criticism makes it almost impossible to acknowledge our gifts and our goodness.

Negative thinking erodes our self-esteem. Expecting the worst seems to attract negative people and situations into our lives. And it's a vicious circle, our negativity weighing us down more and more until it's hard to get up in the morning.

Bringing the sun back into our lives first requires facing the fact that we have a negative attitude. Then we have to learn to listen for the critic and become willing to live with the initial anxiety of silencing him or her. It's not easy to let go.

Replacing negative thoughts with positive affirming ones may at first feel silly or false. That's the critic talking. In time, however, we grow used to them and believe them. Our thoughts, which translate into attitude, can remake us and our lives.

Today, help me identify one negative thought and replace it with a positive one.

August 25

Every man desires to live long but no man would be old.

> *Jonathan Swift*

When asked why his later works had so much more freedom and vigor than his earlier ones, Pablo Picasso replied, "It takes a long time to become young."

In Hunza, a district in northern Pakistan, men and women regularly live past one hundred years of age. An eighty-year-old Hunza ruler had this to say about aging:

The true keynote of life is growth, not aging.
Life does not grow old.
So-called age is the deterioration of enthusiasm, faith to live, and the will to progress.

As we age, internal growth accelerates. The accumulated wealth of our years gives us many perspectives on life. We have learned what's important. We take less for granted.

We are far better equipped to take some risks that youth would not permit. Maybe the stakes feel just as high, but the person we are still becoming knows it's worth it.

Today, let me know that no one ever died of old age.

You can't live in the past. What's gone is gone. I live for today and the future.

Yettie Spiegel

Yettie Spiegel entered the University of Maryland at age 80 because it "made me feel I'm not a time-waster." At 85, she graduated with a bachelor's degree in English and a 3.69 grade point average.

Then there's the salesman who in his twenties gave up his dream of medical school to support his family. When he was 56 he finally entered medical school, figuring that he would be the same age in eight years with or without his medical degree. He retired at 85 after 20 years in a fulfilling and busy practice.

What are we doing today about our life plans and goals? Are we actively working toward a dream? Do we believe we deserve to reach for and attain a special goal? Fear and resignation are poor companions for those of us who want to live life fully. We are never too old to begin following new dreams. The world is waiting for us. As we embrace new possibilities, we grow in happiness and hope.

Today, let me expand my horizons to dream new dreams and consider new plans.

August 27

Those of us who have come to make regular use of prayer would no more do without it then we would refuse air, food, and sunshine.

Bill Wilson

Prayer is the fuel that keeps the hours of our days running smoothly. Those of us who have prayed for years may find that we pray automatically throughout the day. We have ongoing conversations with God.

More often than not, however, our prayers are informal. Since God is with us all day, why wait for a set time and place to pray?

Formal prayer draws upon a deeper part of ourselves. When we are focused on prayer without distractions we are more likely to encounter the deeper feelings which the business of the day has no room for. These feelings, painful or joyful, challenge us to listen rather than speak to God. Thus we receive insight into God's will for us. Disciplined prayer can bring us a peace that prayer on the run cannot.

Formal prayer or meditation lends structure and solace to our busy days. With it we can come to know ourselves and God's will for us more fully.

Today, help me renew my prayer life.

*Rather than tell yourself, "I don't know how
to fully live my life, so I can't commit
myself," commit yourself and then set about
discovering how to do it.*

Peter McWilliams

Risk-takers trust life and themselves enough to
take at least one step into the unknown. Risk-takers
can't predict the future; instead they trust the voice
within that says, "Yes, this is what I am to do next."

As we grow older, we can withdraw and turn in
upon ourselves or we can expand our vision and interests. We might start with a small risk like making a
phone call to get information on a class we think we
might like to take, or planning our next trip by train
rather than plane to discover how it would feel to slow
down and enjoy our own company.

Taking risks, however small, uplifts us. When we
take risks we are in effect deciding not to let our lives
just happen to us. We are deciding to act rather than
react.

Risks teach us about ourselves. As we experience
the challenge of a new project or task, we feel what it's
like to live life rather than watch from the sidelines. It
is impossible to be bored and useless when we risk.

*Today, let me risk doing one small thing I have
dreamed about.*

August 29

If women are sex objects in our culture, men are work objects. They have to be rocks because rocks are predictable and always show up for work on time.

Elissa Melamed

Men are traditionally expected to perform and produce in the workplace. Many become their professional identity; their self-esteem rises and falls with their success or lack of it. They think, "I am as good a person as I am professionally successful." To many men, retirement, job changes, or unemployment means ego-murder.

Who are we without our job? What good are we? What would we do with our days without the routine of work? Do we feel so inadequate when we have work trouble that we are ashamed to talk to anyone about it?

The burden and pressures of being continuously productive can literally wear a person out. Both men and women need to look at the root of our belief that we are what we do. It's in the culture and it's in our families, but we can change it. It won't feel good at first. We may meet with opposition. But acting as if there is more to life than work will gradually make it so.

If we're breathing, we deserve love and many other things. We don't have to do anything for it.

Today, help me get a new perspective on work by talking with someone I trust.

There is no wilderness so terrible, so beautiful, so acid and fruitful as the wilderness of compassion. It is the only desert that shall truly flourish like the lily.

Thomas Mertz

Rewards await those parents who watch with compassion as their young adult children stumble and fall along their life's path. What we must want to do is prevent our child's suffering however we can, but sometimes it's best to stand back and let them figure it out for themselves. Their solutions won't be ours. They will probably be messier, take more time, struggle over obstacles we conquered long ago. But in letting go we give them dignity and the confidence born of hammering out workable solutions.

The faith inherent in our compassion is more healing than the anxious mistrust of a caretaker. When we let go of our children, it is for them; when we hold on, it is for us.

One of the healthiest legacies we can leave our children is the trust we invest in them and the faith we express in the face of life. In this way we teach them that each of us has the gifts to master whatever life hands us.

Today, let me watch with compassion as my children slip and fall and learn about their own resources.

August 31

*Go as far as you can see and by the time
you get there, you'll be able to see farther.*

Melody Beattie

All of us are survivors who have weathered life's storms. Those of us with a little bit of tunnel vision, however, seem to do better than the rest during hard times. The ability to stay focused on the present during hard times diffuses a lot of the dread that worrying about tomorrow brings.

When we were younger, we often resisted life's trials. We thought prayer, wishing, or doing exactly the right thing could and should protect us and those we love from hard times. Now we know better. We know we are powerless over some of the cards life has to deal. We know, too, that the resources and strength that saw us through yesterday's hard times will see us through today's. Surviving dark days has taught us to trust that our resources will continue to work for us.

These resources are the product of our growth, which is the fruit of pain and suffering. They are rocks we can anchor ourselves to, bedrock we can stand on. We can trust them as we trust the sun to rise. We now have money in our internal banks to ride us through hard times.

Today, let me remember that God and I can get through anything life brings.

*I loved sex in my sixties and seventies and I
expect it'll get better as I get older.*

Claude Jones

Masters and Johnson tell us that our desire and
capacity for sexual intimacy continue into our eighties
and nineties and beyond. Growing older need not
mean a loss of sexual fulfillment. Rather, it challenges
us to adjust, physically and emotionally. Where the
bond is less physically intense, it may become more
spiritual, comforting, and healing.

The advantage now and later is that we know ourselves and our needs and our partner's as never before.
We are increasingly aware that our sexuality is not
something separate form the whole of our being.

This awareness can help us let go of old notions
about how we must look and how we must perform. It
can help us discover ourselves and our partners sexually, perhaps for the first time, in ways the anxiety and
self-consciousness of youth would not permit.

Today, let me rethink my attitudes about sexuality.

September 2

The habit of comparing is a dirty trick we play on ourselves and others.

Ruth Appleton

When we compare ourselves with others we often end up holding the short end of the stick. If we were judged as lacking when we were children, it may still be all too easy to do the same to ourselves. Maybe today we are comparing ourselves to someone who is able to give without becoming depleted. We find ourselves buoyed up by them. But then we beat ourselves up for not being good enough.

When we focus on our defects, we're unable to see our assets. Instead of celebrating our gifts, we shame ourselves with supposed shortcomings, often such small ones that they mean little to anyone but us. We each navigate life differently. We are right on course and can trust our progress. Today we are exactly where we need to be, in the center of our own life. When we stop comparing ourselves with others, we are on our way to connecting with them.

Today, help me value my own gifts and trust that I am exactly where I need to be.

There was great passion in my love . . . but
seldom joy. I was devastated by my passion.
I was shattered . . . I had no vision of
myself.

Scott Turow

Joy and hope are the expressions of a growing love relationship. When we respect and are respected in our partnership, we have room to be our true selves. Whenever one partner is stifled, problems will erupt.

Love challenges us to listen and really hear the other, to come to know the other not just as our lover, in relation to us, but as a three-dimensional person in his or her own right. It is a risk to say, "Tell me all about it. I want to know how you feel. I won't punish you with anger or withdraw from you if you risk saying what's on your mind." We might not hear what we want to hear. We might not agree. But we are building a relationship between two whole people. One of the great rewards is that we have a built-in supporter who, knowing our true self, can help us become our best self.

Relationships based on passion, power, and control are relationships based on surfaces, on fantasy and projection. Because they are unreal, with impossible expectations, they go round and round, stuck in blame and defensiveness. Real listening doesn't happen.

Passion may feed the body but compassion feeds the heart. In the heart is where we can be heard.

Today, let me listen to my partner without interrupting to tell him or her how I see it.

September 4

There is no greater refreshment than interior silence and the peace that comes from accessing the divine reservoir of energy within us.

Thomas Keating

Most of us know the time it takes to cultivate an intimate relationship. The same holds true in seeking closer contact with the god of our understanding.

Integrating spiritual practice into our lives takes time. We may at first choke on the words "god" or "prayer." For some of us these words have had little to do with the people we've been.

If we've never prayed before, or haven't since childhood, we may at first feel self-conscious or anxious or silly. Years into the practice we may still feel prayer or meditation to be an awkward fumbling toward grace which is still punctured by our doubt.

But we can persevere. Creative vision, self-healing, reconciliation, the experience of goodness and beauty, hope, and faith-filled action are just some of the fruits of our attempts to commune with the god of our understanding on a regular basis.

Today, let me find my god present within me.

*You know you've reached middle age when
your weightlifting consists merely of standing up.*

Bob Hope

Exercise, proper diet, sleep, relaxation, play, and
rest are essential to a healthy, balanced life. One of the
chief benefits of exercise is stress release.

In our society we see physical deterioration all
around us. It's easy to conclude that such deterioration
is normal and thus inevitable. But it's not. We can
choose health, even to the extent of becoming
healthier than we were in our youth.

Since life is not a course in self-improvement, it's
important that we make changes gradually, and give
ourselves a lot of breaks. One day of not exercising
does not a failure make. Quite the contrary. Taking
a day off here and there can give our muscles a
much-needed rest. It can tell us if we're becoming
compulsive.

Exercise need not become a god. What counts is
that it feels good. It's a tool that can reconnect us with
our bodies and keep us healthy.

Today, let me exercise.

September 6

*What paralyzes life is the failure to believe
and the failure to dare.*

  Pierre Teilhard de Chardin

When we retire our capacity to believe and to take risks we dry up. We lose our zest for life. When we cease to believe in our own dreams and resources, we effectively disconnect ourselves from the revitalizing energy of the earth and the life force that in humans manifests as love. If we are all connected, that connection can sustain us when we cannot sustain ourselves. Shutting the door on our dreams is like turning out the lights of love.

We can be rekindled if we are willing to reach out. A phone call or letter to a friend can do wonders for our sagging spirits. To plug ourselves back into the stream of life we need only connect. The smallest gesture will do it. It is an act of faith to reach out. But we are equal to the challenge. Chances are, only good can come of it.

Today, let me connect with someone I have not spoken to for a long time.

*Healthy guilt leads to remorse but not
self-hate.*

       Judith Viorst

Healthy guilt accepts that we have made some
poor choices and decisions in our lives, but shame says
we make mistakes because we are a mistake. Shame
keeps us stuck in unresolved grief. When we believe
we are bad, we can accept neither healing, forgiveness, nor love in our lives. Instead, we punish ourselves or others, sometimes unmercifully.

Shame keeps us stuck in our pain. It makes us
reject good plans and dismiss optimism. It fosters the
belief that we are utterly powerless to change the circumstances of our lives.

Secrets make us sick, and most secrets are rooted
in shame. Today we can begin to loosen shame's grip
on our lives by sharing one secret with a safe person.
Giving ourselves many daily pats on the back for our
good qualities can also help heal us. Letting go of
shame challenges us to become our own best friend.
Once the weight that is shame begins to lift, new
energy flows into our lives. We can take responsibility
for our mistakes without believing we are a mistake.
We can love ourselves because we are not perfect.

*Today, help me find a safe person to share one of my
shame-filled secrets with.*

September 8

*Experience is the name that every one gives
to his mistakes.*

Oscar Wilde

Of course we make mistakes! Not a day goes by
without our quirky human errors. Our mistakes can be
ignored, acknowledged, or magnified out of proportion. They can be covered up, learned from, cor-
rected, or shrugged off. Mistakes are a springboard for
growth, if we allow them to be. They offer tangible
daily opportunities for honesty and humility. They test
our sense of perfectionism.

Mistakes hurt. It's hard to admit when we're
wrong. But it's harder still to live with the knowledge
when we don't. On some level we know. We can no
longer hide from ourselves.

Acknowledging our mistakes to ourselves or to
another person keeps them and us in perspective.
Acknowledging mistakes builds trust. Making them is
one of life's great equalizers and is the only way we
really learn and grow.

*Today, let me lighten the weight of my error by
acknowledging it.*

*Laughter is the shortest distance between
two people.*

Victor Borge

Have we ever envied someone his or her uninhibited laughter or joy? Have we been drawn in in spite of ourselves? Such good humor is an expression of spirituality anchored in the present.

If we find ourselves attracted to people with happy dispositions, it is a sign we are becoming healthier. We want to be in their presence, even though we may need to be passive observers most of the time. But we are learning that there is a wider perspective on life than just our own, and when we laugh at something that used to be painful, then we are learning what really matters in life.

If nothing else, we can smile. On some days, even if it feels forced, it can lighten our load. Soon smiling becomes habitual, and more happy people are attracted to us. In this way we make our lives different through our own work, and we see the power of a smile, and the power of our effort in our day.

Today, let me appreciate the value of laughter.

September 10

*They started to fight when the money got
tight.*

Billy Joel

Money may become a battleground in intimate
relationships. It is here where power struggles often
get played out, here where issues of control and trust
often rise to the surface. Money can bring out the
worst in us; we fear there is never enough. Since no
two of us would spend it exactly the same way, it's easy
to interpret another's spending habits as a personal
betrayal.

Some of us, however, have learned to cultivate an
attitude of abundance rather than lack. We don't necessarily have more money than others but we have
come to believe our needs will be met. Achieving such
a state requires self-examination. When we fight about
money, what are we really fighting about? Is it a way to
avoid dealing with other issues in the relationship?

Perhaps we need to think about money beyond
considering what it will buy. What beliefs about money
did we inherit from our families, or absorb from the
culture? If these beliefs hurt and oppress us, maybe we
need to rethink them and find a common ground with
our intimates. Money is not a god, but a means of
exchange. It need not rule us. It need not remain a
constant source of fear and anxiety.

*Today, let me get honest about money and refrain from
using it emotionally with those I love.*

September 11

Let there be spaces in our togetherness.
Kahlil Gibran

Shortly after Casey Stengel retired from his position as manager of the New York Yankees, his wife complained, "I married Casey for better or for worse but not for lunch." Even the healthiest relationships can be threatened by the changes in life-style which retirement bring.

Over the years thriving marriages develop their own rhythm. Both partners learn to accommodate the schedules, pace, and interests of the other.

But what happens when we find ourselves face to face with each other all day, every day, when for years we have both been used to our own routine and space. How do we adjust? First we acknowledge that it will take time and that with any change comes growing pains. It's important that we not abandon yesterday's life and the people in it wholesale that we incorporate into today those aspects that meet our needs and bring us pleasure. It's a challenge, but the honesty, creativity, and intimacy of our love will grow if we are willing to sit down at a new "table of life" to plan and negotiate.

Today, let me realize that my marriage can grow only to the extent that I am willing to be honest and open with my partner during times of change.

September 12

*Who, then, can so softly bind up the wound
of another, as he who has felt the same
wound?*

Thomas Jefferson

Our own wounds prepare us to nurse the wounds
of others. In pain we learn compassion and empathy.
The more we confront, feel, and move through our
own pain, the better we can appreciate the depths of
another's suffering.

Pain is the great teacher. In pain we learn our life
lessons. We learn how to be there for others. If suffering does us any good, perhaps it is in how it enlarges
our capacity to open our arms as healers to others.

Wounded healers can sit through the tears and torment of their brothers and sisters, confident that there
is an end to the pain. As we reach out to others in
compassion, we find that our old wounds throb less.
Life has prepared us to better understand the pain of
others, and when we take the time to do so, we are
enriched beyond measure.

*Today, let me know that my life wounds teach me
about empathy and compassion and allow me to reach
out to another.*

Growth demands a temporary surrender of security.

Gail Sheehy

We can't get from one place to another without stepping out on a limb. Limbwalking is a skill we need in order to get on with life. Risking on a dream or idea keeps us vigorous and interesting. The more we challenge our resources and abilities, the greater our measure of joy and satisfaction.

If we don't dare to dream, or risk having to begin again, we may slip into stagnation and depression. Maybe we have never believed we'd be older than thirty-five. Maybe we've never imagined ourselves on the far side of youth, or have seen it only as an absence —an absence of energy, of possibility, of attractiveness.

In coming to terms with our mortality we give life more meaning. We see how essential our ability to dream and take risks really is. Every risk we take renews us. Challenge fires us up in the morning and brings us contentment by evening. Days in which we do something new and daring are God's days.

Today, let me let go of safety and take a risk.

September 14

*Trust is the antidote for fear. Trust that we
will be given everything we need to get
through this moment and this day.*

Murphy Tobin

When left unchecked, fear can become epidemic
in our psyches. One woman was ruled by the conviction that if she stopped adding rooms to her house she
would die. When she died, her house contained 160
rooms, two thousand doors, ten thousand windows,
and covered over six acres of ground.

When fear takes over, we lose our sense of balance, judgment, and humor and become obsessed.
Fear produces dread, which cannot co-exist with joy.
Fear suspends us above any possible joy in the present
and catapults us into a hypothetical future, filled with
dread.

Trust, which is faith, can counteract fear. Fear is
weak in the face of faith, weak in the face of love. We
can practice faith, we can learn to be more present,
but sometimes we need other people to remind us of
this. Beyond fear's function of alerting us to danger,
we don't need it to be a constant refrain in our lives.
We can live quite well without it.

*Today, let me remember that future events are not real
and help me release one fear.*

No man can become a saint in his sleep.

Henry Drummond

Action is life's magic word. We've all heard the saying, "a journey of a thousand miles begins with a single step," but sometimes we feel overwhelmed. We believe there is so much wrong in our lives. Where do we start to fix the mess? Some of us become paralyzed and do nothing because the task seems so big.

There once was a woman who had a very dirty house. Every morning she got up and looked around and felt so guilty and helpless that she put off cleaning for yet another day. The higher the piles of dirt rose, the worse she felt. Finally, a neighbor suggested that she would eventually have a clean house if she cleaned one room at a time.

Maybe one room is too much. If so, we can take a corner of it or part of a corner. We can spend half an hour or five minutes, whatever feels manageable. It's amazing what a tonic action can be, however small.

Today, help me separate my problems and tackle one of them.

September 16

Life is not a dress rehearsal.
Beth Beermann

Let us take an inventory of our stock-of-life; we alone are accountable for the contents. Are we still trying to make the best of a distasteful job, a dull marriage, an unpleasant locality? Why have we settled for such mediocrity? Has a sense of duty kept us here?

What ever happened to the ambition, yearnings, once-blooming talents we had years ago, when all of life seemed ahead of us? How did we get sidetracked? We may have some security now, yet our lives are predictable and, at times, quite uninspiring. We wait for vacations or look to retirement before our "real" lives resume.

Let us look at ourselves as the protagonist in a play. Has the action become so monotonous that we yawn as we review it?

In our inventory we will find many things to be proud and grateful for. A written list of new challenges and goals may be all we need to spur us on to greater satisfaction and fulfillment, so the drama that is our lives may continue.

Today, let me assess Act II and rewrite the script for Act III.

*The paired butterflies are already yellow
with August over the grass in the west garden. They hurt me. I grow older.*

   T'Ai-Po Li

We have been powerful people in our lives, but
never powerful enough to stop time and the pull of
gravity. We dream while the clock ticks. Why is it that
when we really begin to appreciate life, its ending
haunts us? At some point, the balance shifts and we
find that our memories may outnumber our dreams.

Memories can both hurt and evoke joy. As we
grow older life grows bittersweet. "I don't ever
remember it being this lovely," we say of each new season.

How can we accept aging yet not give up on our
dreams? By continuing to take risks. By acknowledging that the wealth of years we've lived—our very age
—is what enables us to feel so deeply. Age changes our
perspective. We take less for granted.

This perspective can dissolve the obstacles of the
past. It can help us act with greater conviction. It can
remind us we are never too old to dream.

*Today, let me experience the bittersweet edge of my life
and grow with it.*

September 18

I could dance with you till the cows come home. Better still, I'll dance with the cows and you come home.

Groucho Marx

For many of us, our days of burning the candle at both ends are about over. Staying out all night now means a morning when no amount of caffeine can repair the damage done. Our bodies bear eloquent testimony.

We've raised our share of hell; let's leave it now to another generation. Today freshness of attitude rather than long hours and crazy behavior can better serve the people we are becoming.

Moderation is more than an idea. It is a reality our bodies and minds respond to. When we find ourselves back on the edge—which for many of us means not getting the rest, nutrition, support, or space we need— it's easy to forget how something as simple as eight hours of sleep can repair and renew us. Simple self-care can banish many of the demons that plague us. It can remind us that achieving serenity today need not be a mammoth undertaking but is within easy reach.

Today, let me see the sanity of not getting too hungry, angry, lonely, or tired.

*Seeing . . . I believe that the whole of life
consists in that verb.*

      Pierre Teilhard de Chardin

Life is best lived somewhere midway between
yielding and rigidity. To strike that fine balance we
need to continually let go and see.

We need to let go of outcomes, and of our reliance
on them as indicators of our self-worth. We need to
surrender our vision of ourselves as all-powerful and
thus all-responsible for whatever happens to ourselves
and to our loved ones. We need to reconnect with the
real abiding power we do have, which, like a fine web,
spans the distance from yielding to rigidity and
excludes neither.

Centering and thus seeing requires the great sen-
sitivity many of us have muffled with thick skins. Perhaps we no longer need such rigorous protection.
Perhaps we can risk coming out from under, the better
to use our sixth sense. That sense would have us flow
with, rather than against, life. It would have us know
peace rather than strife.

*Today, let me believe that vision, prosperity, and peace
will be mine when I am willing to give up my role as
Captain of the Life Ship.*

September 20

Actions can be good or bad. People only good.

Anthony de Mello

Life is easier for those of us who begin each day with the belief that people are basically good. Belief in this basic goodness allows us to believe the same thing about ourselves.

Some would call us Pollyannas for believing in this essential goodness. They'd say we're out of touch with reality. But whose reality? Deciding to seek out the good in someone does not mean denying or minimizing actions that may be bad. It means choosing to focus attention on the positive. It means giving power of influence in our lives to good things rather than bad. It means glorifying the gold rather than the garbage—because we don't have the time to do both. It is in fact easier to take our own measure where our actions are concerned once we've learned not to condemn the actor.

We can choose to be prospectors for goodness. The specks of gold we find will outshine all the rocks we step over on the way to our treasure.

Today, let me look for the good in myself and others.

*Worry builds mountains of fear and humor
changes these mountains into manageable
hills.*

                    John Wilson

Each day during a long hospital stay, Joe received
several letters. When a fellow patient noticed the large
volume of mail, Joe explained that every day he wrote
and mailed letters to himself. In these letters he listed
in detail his every worry and fear. Then he mailed the
letters to an old address, knowing they wouldn't be
forwarded to him for at least a week. In this way Joe
learned to let go and laugh at his worries. Most of
them never came true.

Worry, like cigarette smoking, can be addictive. It
can become so interwoven into the fabric of our day
that we hardly notice it. When we step back and take
note of our thoughts, when we listen to what is really
going on in there, we often find that it's mostly static
and old tapes, baggage from the past. We can choose
not to listen to it. Like Joe, we can let our worries run
their course without believing in their dire forecast.

*Today, let me lighten up and realize that most of my
worries won't actually happen.*

September 22

No man can think clearly when his fists are clenched.

George Jean Nathan

Unchecked aggression destroys. If we find ourselves plagued by aggressive behaviors and temper tantrums our relationships are probably in quicksand. Acting out through verbal or physical violence erodes the hearts and spirits, if not the bodies, of those we love and increases our isolation, shame, and loneliness.

If we observed our parents or caretakers connect only in anger, we learned that anger equals intimacy. There are other ways. Changing aggressive behavior into assertive behavior is necessary if we want to grow emotionally and spiritually and be in relationships with loving people.

Many of us have changed our most negative behavior by admitting we have a problem and being willing to change. Willingness and the wish to live a better life can turn around the most difficult situation. We may need professional help to change deep-seated aggressive behavior; but getting humble and honestly asking for help are the first steps. In moving beyond anger as a way of life, we discover real intimacy. We find out that real connections can only happen without the volume turned up.

Today, let me take responsibility for my anger.

*Well, I'm happy tonight. I'm not worried
about anything. I'm not fearing any man.*
                    Martin Luther King, Jr.

Deep within, we are always safe, always protected, always loved. Those of us who have not yet
realized this truth need only venture into the realm of
the spirit, where the god of our understanding offers us
freedom from fear. Nothing and no one can harm us in
the center of our being. It is truly ours to own. We are
safe here.

But how do we get there? Perhaps all our lives we
were told no such place exists, or if it does, that it's out
there, outside us. Getting there now takes time,
patience, commitment, and faith. It means cultivating
an awareness of the voice within that may be barely a
whisper. It means trusting that voice. No easy task, but
if we're alive there is such a voice, however faint.

We have days when we can't hear it, but our
Higher Power always can. If we can remember only
this, we can know safety. We can know freedom from
fear.

Today, let me hear and trust my inner voice.

September 24

*There are but three things that can be done
about reaching middle age; deny it, proceed
directly to old age, or live with it—and the
latter is best accomplished through laughter.*

Clarence Petersen

If we've never laughed at ourselves, it's high time
we learned how. Foibles we once scrambled to cover,
foibles that ruled us because we took them so seriously,
need no longer paralyze us. It's not easy to take back
the power they've had over us. But now, with the perspective of age, perhaps we can allow that they've
done some good. They've kept us humble, made us
empathetic, connected us with the next person, who
struggles just as we do. Happily, we are flawed.

About a week before his death at the age of 100,
Eubie Blake said: "If I'd known I was gonna live this
long, I'd have taken better care of myself." With that
attitude, it sounds like he took great care of himself.
He knew how to laugh.

Today, let me take excellent care of myself by laughing.

The final power is to be at home with powerlessness.

Anthony de Mello

Life continually challenges us to let go and accept powerlessness, especially when we are hurting. Especially when we want most to believe that we have some control, that life is not some fool's game, utterly out of our hands.

So we fight. Whether passively or aggressively, we're poised for the next attack. Some of us withdraw from life. Some of us go back out. But we're guarded, contracted in fear, and thus equally isolated. We are wary lest what power we believe we possess would be taken from us.

To become open to trust and love in the face of pain and grief is the great challenge of faith. To acknowledge our limits, to know, finally, that we can't cover all the bases, is to know what we can cover. Once freed from the delusion that we are all-powerful, we find greater comfort inside our own lives. We find the strength and power that comes, not from straining, but from surrender.

Today, let me trust God's plan for me

September 26

I feel fortunate to have come to that time in life when I can finally enjoy what my Quaker grandmother would have called "peace at the center."

Richard M. Nixon

Can we see down the road to what truly counts? What if we're now in our eighties or nineties, looking back? What would we have wished to do differently? What would stand out as important? Perhaps we need to experience a bit of prestige or applause to realize how transient and hollow it can be, how short-lived its satisfaction. What we may be seeking is something deeper, but we don't know how to get it.

Once we perceive peace as important, as a worthy goal, ways of achieving it will open up to us. Whether person, place, or thing, they may have been right in front of us all along. But in our rush to become, we could not see them or passed them over.

When we come to believe we deserve peace, it won't be something we have to carve out of our lives from scratch, alone. We'll attract what and who we need to achieve it.

Today, let me be willing to make room in my life for peace.

We are a nation obsessed with losing weight.
Yet most of the time, this excess weight
that's between us and perfection isn't even
on our bodies—it's in our heads.

    Moira Bailey

Do we see ourselves as others see us? Sometimes. Maybe. Maybe we need to rethink our notions about, if not our quest for, the ideal size and shape. Even if we are able and willing to spend lots of money in the pursuit of losing or gaining extra pounds, there are countless traps in seeking and maintaining physical excellence. Weight and body shape mean something different to us now than they did 25 years ago.

If we're compulsive about eating or obsessed with our weight, chances are there's something deeper at issue. Obsessions and compulsions can be signposts, our body's way of signaling trouble elsewhere. It's important to talk about this, to find out we're not alone, to find out that the perfect body cannot make us whole or heal us.

Being conscientious about our weight or health is different from being obsessed with it. We need not be ruled by the numbers on the scale. Rather than fighting our bodies we can learn to join forces with them.

Today, help me know if my concern about my weight or health is obscuring a deeper issue.

September 28

I'd learned long ago that being Lewis Carroll was infinitely more exciting than being Alice.

Joyce Carol Oates

Although we may be squarely planted in our lives we can learn from lives we will never live. We can be enriched by fiction we have not created. There is a place for us.

Maybe we have scaled down our notions of what we would become, what our role in life would be. Maybe our need to be center stage has diminished. It does not mean our gifts, our talents, are any less, or that we are any less. It means that we've grown into who we were meant to become.

It can be a great relief to know our limitations, to know where we belong. To know where we belong is to know, with some certainty, where satisfaction if not happiness can be found. Right here.

Today, let me believe that I am who I was meant to be.

*It is prudent to pour the oil of delicate
politeness on the machinery of friendship.*

       Colette

Inviting friends to share a simple meal or gathering a few folks for a spontaneous party reminds us how important hospitality is as a way of demonstrating our care for others. Friendships deepen with generosity.

In mid-life we may be looking to solidify our friendships. Even if we are blessed with a multitude of kinfolk, our non-family friends are essential. They enrich us; they encourage our growth. We need to nurture these precious relationships, for we will rely on them more in the years to come.

Hospitality can be learned. With practice it can become second nature, a comfortable way of giving of ourselves. In return, we will become confident in our ability to sustain old friendships. A social life of our own making keeps us vital, keeps us connected to the larger world beyond ourselves.

Today, let me welcome my friends.

September 30

Jiminy Cricket was my first philosophical hero.

Willard Scott

Pinocchio may have personified honesty and conscience. It seemed so natural then. Since then some of us have lost sight of these values. Expediency worked well; no one questioned us. Some of us learned to ignore our conscience and became masters at rationalizing our dishonesty.

Today we may yearn for authenticity, for honesty. We may want the truth at all costs. Lying and equivocating once may have been necessary to survive. But we are stronger now. We no longer need lies to protect us or please someone else. Now, too, we are in a better position to see and know what is true.

Honesty is a skill that can be waxed forth, learned. It may not always feel comfortable or appropriate, but speaking our own truths makes it easier to live with ourselves. Honesty can keep us whole.

Today, let me speak the truth fearlessly.

Some children hear their parents scolding them from the grave, like a "ghost of Christmas past" in Dickens.
Harold Ivan Smith

Coming to terms with our parents is part of our agenda as adults. If we are burdened with uncertainties, prejudices, and frustrated wishes, our parents, whether alive or dead, still may be holding us hostage in the form of the messages they gave us.

Many of us have a distorted sense of loyalty to our parents. They may evoke fear, shame, and powerlessness in us. Parents long dead can still haunt us. They can still, at the slightest trigger, rouse guilt or shame.

Counseling can help us see our parents for who they are, who they wanted to be, who they could never be—especially to us. We can become free from our emotional dependence on them, from needing their approval. We can learn to get our needs met by those who can meet them.

Once we see them for who they are, we will gradually stop expecting the impossible from them. When we let them be, they will have less power over us. They can let us be.

Today, help me let my parents be, warts and all.

October 2

For some on the road to the golden years, a move can be one of life's great adventures. It can be a renaissance.

Kent Collins

If done impulsively, a move at mid-life can signal confusion and internal chaos. Done thoughtfully, however, moving to another part of the country can show us our adaptability, strength, and independence.

The thought of making a geographical change may appear unexpectedly. It may seem impetuous. It need not be. The thought may spring from a real need to shift gears and go forward.

Today, feeling self-reliant may out-weigh a house full of sentiment. This need mean no disrespect to our past, only that our priorities have shifted. We can take our memories with us. We may want the set of fresh possibilities a new location presents.

Well-meaning adult children cannot know what is best for us. Though they may not like this disruption in their version of us, they cannot keep us from going. When we are ready, we can go. We can be secure in the knowledge that we know what we need, that we alone know what is best for us.

Today, let me contemplate what a move might mean to me.

*If we don't sleep for a night or two, no
harm will come unless we try too hard.
So don't try to force sleep.*

        Earl Ubell

Insomnia can be frightening. At 3:30 a.m., still
wide awake, we may feel confused, paralyzed with
fears. Our stability may seem endangered. Are we
going mad?

We may ask ourselves if this is medical or emotional, yet delay resolving the question. We may resort
to sleeping pills. The hangovers that result, however,
can be more troublesome than the night hours spent
lying awake.

If during the day we have courage to talk about
the fear, guilt, or bitterness we may be feeling about
the people and situations we can't control, we will
have taken the first step toward clearing our psyches
for the blessed relief of sleep. No one ever died from
lack of sleep, it is said. When we are honestly willing
to stop tormenting ourselves, rest will return.

*Today, let me live this day well and accept the results
tonight.*

October 4

Healthy guilt is the remorse we feel when we hurt ourselves or someone else. It is good because it teaches us conscience and compassion. If we're willing to learn from it we get wise.

Joan Borysenko

Guilt isn't always bad; it can keep us in line and point us in the right direction. If we feel guilty, perhaps we are. Yet we may feel guilty when we're not meeting someone else's expectations. This harmful, misplaced guilt is more the result of perfectionism. If we are full of self-criticism, blaming ourselves night and day until we have lost sight of anything other than our failures, then we are far beyond healthy guilt.

We may need help in figuring out what we can change in our lives, and what is beyond our control. Once we do this, however—once we define the areas in which we are responsible—we can act on them and let go of the rest. The rest is the burden of unhealthy guilt. When we come to accept ourselves as fallible human beings, our obsessive guilt will dissolve.

Today, let me forgive myself for not being perfect and start to let go of guilt.

*The final moment of assuming adulthood
may be when we inherit the legacy, become
keeper of traditions, the curator of our
family's past and future memories.*

        Ellen Goodman

Holidays are now spent at our homes; family reunions are held at our insistence. We observe anniversaries, graduations, marriages, births, deaths —adding our own traditions to those passed down by our elders.

Traditions hold families together over time and through the generations. By upholding them we nurture our roots. If we refuse to accept this role, the traditions may disappear, and with them a certain knowledge of ourselves that can only be gained by knowing where we come from. To reject the past and its traditions wholesale is to reject a part of ourselves, part that we'll no longer have the tools to understand should we ever want to.

Traditions are not just handed down but taken up consciously. They confer not only continuity and community, but self-knowledge.

Today, let me scrutinize my past for what among it I can pass on.

October 6

*After the first couple of thousand orgasms
in life, the whole business seems to lose
some of the urgency associated with it in
earlier years.*

                    Fred Schoenberg

When we were younger we may have insisted on
immediate gratification when it came to sex. We may
have defined sex or sexuality as something we do
rather than something we are.

Now we can entertain a wider definition. It can
include passionate living. Sexuality is whole body. It is
the life of the senses; it is the desire to create. Our sexuality is our feelings, however, wherever, they are
expressed.

We are fully attractive human beings; every twinkle in our eyes tells us that we are still sexual, sensual
beings. We can enjoy our middle-age sexuality
whether or not we have an active sex life.

Today, let me know myself to be a sexual being.

*People who are in need and are not afraid
to beg give to people not in need the occa-
sion to do good for goodness' sake. The
Greeks use to say that people in need are
ambassadors of the gods.*

Peter Maurin

When we are presented with an opportunity to
help a fellow human being in need, we have a choice.
Each situation is different and demands its own
response. To make rules for ourselves when it comes to
helping people helps no one.

We help ourselves, however, when we face our
feelings (without judging them) about a given situation
—whether or not we choose to help. And we help the
one in need when we see him or her not as part of a
social problem but as one human being in need. Just
like we are, or have been, or could be.

We can't help everyone. But we can help one. The
way we help ourselves.

*Today, may I remember that "There but for the grace
of God go I."*

October 8

Life itself is the proper binge.
Julia Child

Those of us who are recovering from an addiction or from an addictive relationship get to try on a new approach to living. An approach that not only can manage the unmanageable—our addiction itself—but can change our world into a place we never would have believed possible. If we don't try it, however, it's highly likely we will return to our addiction for relief.

What a prescription to receive at mid-life! Our addiction had us engulfed in a world of unreality; it distorted our perceptions, kept us in despair. How can all of this be changed?

By working a program of recovery and relying on a Power greater than ourselves. Our program must be used, however, not just evaluated or analyzed or passively accepted. When we follow these simple directions we begin to get high on living itself.

Sober, clean, or abstinent, we see life differently. It's a second chance to straighten out our relationships, clear away the wreckage of our past, and rely on the Higher Power who has been with us all along.

Today, let me feel the vitality of my recovery.

*The arena for transformation is daily life,
action, what the daily round of commitments brings us to day after day.*

 Thomas Keating

To experience the divinity in every person and
event, we need the faith born of a solid spiritual base
to see through appearances. We may want so much to
believe that everything in our lives happens for a purpose, and that all is as it should be. First, however, we
need an active relationship with the god of our understanding. It is first in this relationship that comfort,
meaning, and purpose lay.

If we find mid-life to be a chore—trying, painful,
boring, routine—perhaps we are looking for someone
or something to transform our days rather than seeing
ourselves as the place where transformation must
begin. We can look to others for instruction, for guidance, for support—but one day we step out alone.

We know people to whom each day is a gift. If we
want it enough and do the footwork, we, too, can be
transformed.

*Today, let me be conscious of the divine reservoir of
energy within me.*

October 10

Self-pity in its early stages is as snug as a feather mattress. Only when it hardens does it become uncomfortable.

Maya Angelou

A "poor me" attitude implies we've been absorbed in ourselves. This can happen to the best of us when we're sick or when we feel thwarted in getting what we believe we deserve. We say: it is, of course, everyone else's fault.

We may compare ourselves unfavorably to others, and pity ourselves. We may envy those who appear to have more or those who appear to have a life with fewer problems. None of us lack! We may not yet know how to plumb the riches middle age has to offer, but we can learn.

We can begin to untangle ourselves from our feelings of worthlessness by taking action. Our wounded egos can grow strong once we focus away from them. If it means asking for help, we can do that, too. Movement may be what we least feel we can do, but each step after the first is easier. And the benefits of the first can be instantaneous.

Today, let me be released from the tangle of feeling sorry for myself, and move on to hopeful, constructive attitudes.

Origins and destinations and all
Convoluted pathways in between
Did not define you.

    Margaret Allen

Those of us who have attended class reunions may have been shocked at how different yet the same our classmates seemed.

We may remember the school yearbook's prediction of our future. How differently have our lives unfolded? At mid-life, can we hear what we're saying about ourselves to others? Do we know who we are? Do we defend, exaggerate, make excuses for ourselves?

We may be shaken into the awareness that we are not yet who we want to be, that we don't want to meet the same person in the mirror at the next reunion. Now, however, we have the tools for change we've never had before. Now we can change.

Today, let me know that what I've done or where I've been need not restrict my present or future.

October 12

Risk is what separates the good part of life from the tedium.

Jimmy Zero

Some of us have made a career out of giving to others, and at mid-life are caught up short when asked what we enjoy. We have dedicated our lives to serving those in need—children, patients, spouses, employers. We have shrugged off our own pleasure.

Maybe we don't think of ourselves as martyrs. Maybe we never complain. But have we examined our motives?

Now's the time to gamble on ourselves. Authentic love of self includes the risk of self-fulfillment. Gradually, we can learn to enjoy ourselves, to relish those experiences we once would have avoided or prohibited.

We may surprise ourselves to find fulfillment is worth the risk.

Today, let me do something different, something that I enjoy, just for myself.

It's not how much money you have but what you do with it. The joy of living is incredible. We work hard at the things we have to do, so why not take time to enjoy the things we want to do?

Malcolm Forbes

In mid-life, many of us have not yet learned how to take pleasure in our lives. We have spent years achieving or caring for others, doing what family or society has expected of us.

Maybe we have been afraid to discover what gives us enjoyment. Our routine obligations to family and work, while predictable, are secure. Security, however, can lapse into complacency. We can forget that there are other ways to live.

Let us make a few changes. Each day can contain one event that delights us. It is within our power to seek out moments to savor, to take time for the people who encourage us to break away from our routine.

Our daily or weekly inventory can include what we do for pleasure. We can learn to treat ourselves well.

Today, let me find pleasure.

October 14

*In moments of crisis our thoughts do not
run consecutively but rather sweep over us
in waves of intuition and experience.*

John LeCarre

Let us trust ourselves; our instincts are right on target. Even when we are confronted by a totally bizarre set of circumstances, even when we are frightened into a state of near panic, our instincts will enable us to do the right thing.

Our many years of experience will not desert us in a crisis. We have dealt with and resolved challenges of all sorts. In mid-life we are equipped to deal with whatever comes down the pike.

New hurdles can appear unexpectedly; radical, dramatic changes can catch us off guard. Sometimes the rug is pulled from beneath us so suddenly that we do stumble and fall. Once in a while we may feel jaded and battle-weary from pain and distress. During these times, however, we can take pride in our wisdom, our good judgment, our know-how. Mid-life may contain some major surprises, but we have the experience to endure and rebound all the more wiser.

Today, let me believe in the order in chaos, and not expect rational or logical resolutions.

*Life is to live and life is to give and talents
are to use for good if you choose . . . Every
day you shall wonder at yourself, at the
richness of life which has come to you by
the grace of God.*

　　　　　Solanus Casey

Those most spiritually alive are those who glow
with joy. Joy enters when we are open to it—when we
believe we deserve it, when we trust that it can find us.
Today we are capable of this. We can remember when
we have felt centered and whole, and in remembering
invoke it. This attitude enables us to see events and circumstances from a new perspective; negatives can be
transformed by enthusiasm.

By mid-life, we've all experienced joy. We may
yearn for more. Our spiritual center is a wellspring of
life within us. When we allow ourselves to be in touch
with it, we are radiantly, gloriously alive. When we are
attuned to the presence of God within us, we are open
to wisdom and thus to joy.

Today, let me feel joy.

October 16

*My Higher Power has done for me again
what I could not do for myself . . . Fear of
the future was lifted.*

Cynthia Huff

Turning to a Power greater than ourselves can produce the miracle no human can. At mid-life our understanding of God need no longer contain the images and beliefs of childhood. We can reinvent, if we must, a god of our own understanding.

We can risk such a spiritual awakening. As we come to trust our connection with god, as we refer to the god of our understanding more and more, we become stronger and clearer from the inside out. We can expect miracles.

Our faith will change us. We may reverence silence in a new way. We may be drawn to periods of silent prayer. Our actions become more and more continuous with our beliefs. We become able to express love spontaneously. We become aware of our many blessings, talents, and gifts and can feel grateful for the adventure that is our lives.

Today, let my fears be replaced with faith.

*Autumn arrives in the early morning, but
spring at the close of a winter day.*
        Elizabeth Bowen

Fall is when we harvest our memories, when we
wake up under crisp, cool sheets on an October morning. Fall is walking again, quickening our steps on a
country morning. The earth is crunchy under our feet.
We may remember other autumns, other mornings like
this. Looking up, we may have to shield the sun from
our eyes to see the perfect flight formation of the Can-
ada geese. Cooking cinnamon apples on the stove and
selecting that pumpkin that's just right also link us to
the season.

Reflection may be our silent partner as the seasons change. We struggle to let go of the old to make
way for the new. Life and autumn teach us that nothing stays the same. But change comes easier when we
cease to resist it.

Autumn teaches hope as she shuts down, turns off
her colors, and goes underground. Autumn's hope is
for spring, which will come again.

*Today, let me believe that change will lead me to new
solutions and great joy.*

October 18

The most delightful advantage of being bald
—one can hear snowflakes.

R.G. Daniels

If we choose, we can change the way we see and think about even the most mundane aspects of middle age. Our culture tells us a man with a receding hairline or a woman with age wrinkles can no longer be sexy. It says that middle-age spread requires a diet and a health club. It snickers as our bodily strength, endurance, and agility begin to wane.

We do experience these things, they are inevitable, and if we cringe and hide we perpetuate what we know to be a shallow prejudice. Humor can arm us with rejoinders. We are reflective, not slow; we ask you to repeat your question not because we didn't quite hear, but because you must be sure you want our answer!

We need not be governed by ageist, sexist notions of strength and beauty. We can see ourselves clearly and know we are okay. The mirror can tell us so in the new language we've come to learn. The voice that returns the compliment is none other than our own.

Today, help me accept my face, my body—my physical self.

*This is much better than any of the other
marriages. There's really no comparison.*

Lee Nelson Porter

Can remarriage in mid-life be successful? Yes,
indeed! With some maturity and mistakes under our
belts, we can approach a new marriage more accepting of flaws—our own and our partner's. Maybe we
have revised our earlier notions of marriage and
romance and have tossed out the myth of the ideal
spouse. We no longer expect to be saved from ourselves, or have our imperfections complemented by
another's strengths. We want to be needed yet not
smothered.

Now we are more interdependent and determined
to concentrate on the good. We have developed a
healthy sense of humor and value marriage as a desir-
able way of life.

We've learned how to let go of old ideas of how
our new spouse "should" think, feel, act—for this
partner will not follow our scripts. We are relieved at
the freedom and independence we have within this
new marriage, to grow, make choices, to care deeply,
to share, to nurture each other.

Remarriage can renew our trust in our ability to
sustain a relationship with quality companionship, a
sense of comfort, and genuine love.

*Today, let me appreciate the risk and adventure of
mid-life remarriage.*

October 20

It seems to me that the earth may be borrowed but not bought. It may be used, but not owned . . . . We are tenants and not possessors.

Marjorie Kinnan Rawlings

Nature's seasons teach us about the transitory aspects of our own lives. Each period gives way to the next; each contains a time of preparation, ripening, maturing, and dying. The brilliant barrenness and cold of winter fades and is transformed by spring breezes. Life returns. Those who live on the land learn to trust its seasons. They tend the soil and harvest its abundance. They let the earth die back.

As with nature, our old behaviors and perceptions give way to new ones. We must let go of the old to be receptive to the new. When we cling to habits and beliefs that served us well in our younger days, and do not reexamine them, we are out of sync with the cycle.

The progression of the seasons reminds us, in mid-life, that change is constant, healthy, and inevitable. We are temporary tenants, yet there is beauty in our transience.

Today, let me remember that, "To every thing there is a season."

You will do foolish things, but do them with enthusiasm.

        Colette

What if, the next time we see a middle-aged person doing something we think is silly, we refrained from reproach and instead smiled in appreciation? A little silliness now and then is good for us.

When our lives are proceeding too smoothly, we may be saying no to challenges. At mid-life we can ill afford to become timid and shy.

The yearning to explore and enjoy the variety the world has to offer is a blessing. To express the underdeveloped parts of ourselves may mean being ridiculous or appearing rash or ludicrous, but if we don't try it we'll never know. When we do we deserve congratulations.

If we feel stale and weary, perhaps we need some absurdity and nonsense to revive the child in us.

Today, let me salute myself when I'm being a bit zany.

October 22

*If I can't remember something, is it
Alzheimer's? If my bones creak, is it
osteoporosis? If my cholesterol is up,
is the end near?*

Barbara Reynolds

Worry, worry, worry, as though we can control or
avoid this aging process? Why are we still counting
birthdays, measuring, now that probably one-half or
two-thirds of our lifetime is behind us? Have we hoped
all along we would be exempt from growing old?

We can learn not to worry by learning to live one
day at a time. When we do what is in front of us, to the
best of our ability, we need no longer fret about our age.

We can savor any one thing at a time, experience
only one thing at a time, achieve only one thing at a
time. When we concentrate on the moment we're
experiencing, we can defuse our fears about the past or
the future. We can leave yesterday behind, where it
belongs, and need not concern ourselves with tomorrow until it arrives.

Every moment lived well is sufficient in itself.
Aging then becomes irrelevant.

*Today, let me pack joy and riches into these twenty-
four hours.*

When I was in my 20s, I was obsessed with how I looked and the idea of getting older was terrifying. Now I find it rather fascinating. Our battle scars, our wrinkles or whatever, should be looked upon with pride.

Richard Chamberlain

Many of us in our middle years try to deny the changes in our appearance. Some of us go to lengths to prevent or hide the beginning of our physical decline. Coloring our hair, special diets, body building—these stop-the-clock measures in the end can defeat us.

Eventually we will be devastated if our sense of self is determined solely by our appearance. The onus is on us to find role models defined rather by character. They are out there. We are also challenged to shift our focus more toward the inner dimensions of our lives.

If we attend to those dimensions in ourselves we are more likely to know them in others. We can derive great comfort from turning away from the standards of a culture that so favors youth. When that culture no longer defines us we are free to define ourselves. Free, too, to look however we feel.

Today, let me re-create my image of myself.

October 24

*The past is what you remember, imagine
you remember, convince yourself you
remember, or pretend to remember.*

Harold Pinter

Memory is not a file cabinet stored with facts that
can be instantly retrieved, or a video recorder with
instant replay. Our memories sit down through time,
edited here, highlighted there.

We have only to reminisce about childhood with
others who were there to find out how subjective memory can be. Each of us no doubt has a very different
version of any event. Memories are selective, partial,
colored by who we are today.

We view the past through attitudes and beliefs we
hold in the present. Where once all may have looked
grim, it now need not. When we accept and embrace
our past, we need not dismiss the whole for its parts.
We can remember all of it—the good and bad. One
need not spoil the memory of the other.

*Today, let me realize my present is infinitely more
important than my past.*

*Real friends hold us together when times
are tough, and help us rejoice when they're
good again.*

    Niki Scott

To have a friend is to be a friend, and at mid-life
we may want to rearrange our priorities to make some
time for friends. Maybe we've drifted apart from our
once-strongest, most loyal companions. They were
crowded out by our jobs, children, homes, spouses,
and aspirations.

Maybe we feel the urge to renew our acquain-
tance with the people who shared a meaningful part
of our history. A simple phone call can begin the
process.

Time for our old friends must be committed and
scheduled. The advocate and comrade we were to one
another in our youth can become so again, through
mid-life and into old age.

Today, let me renew an old friendship.

October 26

And then, not expecting it, you become
middle-aged and anonymous. No one
notices you. You achieve a wonderful free-
dom. It is a positive thing. You can move
about, unnoticed and invisible.

       Doris Lessing

Mid-life can free us. Released from our constant involvement with our children, relinquishing to the young the pressures of career-climbing, we have more choices. Our time is much more our own.

There's a lot to feel good about. We've achieved a certain level of practical wisdom, distilled from 40-50-60 years of living. We've met substantial challenges and survived. We understand and accept our bodies to a greater degree. We have grown from the responsibilities given to us.

We need no longer be in the spotlight—it blinds us now when we are. We'd rather play to an audience of one.

Today, let me feel the freedom I have.

*One of the many things nobody ever tells
you about middle age is that it's such a nice
change from being young.*
        Dorothy Canfield Fisher

Truthfully, which of us would choose to be 21
again? We may have had tight skin, naivete, fearless-
ness, style—but how silly and shallow much of it
seems now. Our grey hairs and wrinkles are badges of
our achievements, our patience, our endurance. We
can act with informed judgment. We have developed a
manner, skill, and grace all distinctly our own. We
have skill and ingenuity in abundance compared to our
younger counterparts.

We need not envy the young; we've gained more
than we've lost over the years. Our development is full
and mature; it feels right to be an adult. Our experiences have made us proud, and we can look ahead
confident of more.

Today, let me appreciate my middle age.

October 28

*In the Street of "By-and-By," one arrives at
the house of Never.*

Cervantes

Until we learn to dissolve the fears, dislikes, and
doubts that immobilize us and lead us to procrastinate,
we will continue to put off the things that need doing.
Every day we choose. Sometimes we prefer to live
with the guilt, anxiety, and panic that can result from
procrastination. There are a thousand reasons we post-
pone or neglect our obligations. Perhaps if we stop to
ask "why am I doing this?" we will have taken the
first step toward eliminating procrastination.

When we encourage rather than disparage ourselves and acknowledge every small success, we will
come to find ourselves capable of doing anything. We
can begin by saying no to the things that would overload us and yes to what we really want.

*Today, let me realize that eliminating procrastination
is a do-it-myself project that I can choose to put off
until next year.*

*What happens as a matter of maturing is
that . . . you tend to be more forgiving of
people who don't agree with you.*
        Billy Joel

Needing to be right is a hallmark of youth—
necessary, perhaps, in carving out an identity. By mid-
life, however, we have learned that opinions other than
our own are equally valid. We continue to have strong
opinions, yet we need not be pompous about them. We
can listen to another person expound on an issue dear
to our hearts and not label them "too liberal" or "mis-
guided" or "wrong." We no longer need to become
irate or defensive. We are not the sole arbiter of what is
right and wrong, correct and incorrect.

Today, tolerance and patience are what we need
most to build good relationships. Maybe our egos no
longer need constant feeding. We are more secure, not
so threatened when another disagrees with us. "Live
and let live" can be our motto. We can welcome diver-
sity of opinion as the spice of mid-life.

Today, let me live and let live.

October 30

If love is the answer, will you please
rephrase the question?

Lily Tomlin

Answers to our most difficult questions often come to us in the simplest form: "God"; "happiness"; "love." Maybe we are restless with these answers. They aren't what we want to hear. So we dive back into the maze that is our mind to find the answer that will satisfy. An answer that works for one of us may not work for another.

This is our challenge: to find out what bothers us, what makes us uncomfortable, and to phrase it as a question. Some of us write them down in notebooks, set them aside, and later find out that the answers had already materialized. The important thing, we found, was formulating the question.

Answers to the most difficult life situations will come. Let us learn to trust our process: all the answers lie within; no other person can provide them for us.

Today, help me find the right questions.

*You can have anything you want if you want
it desperately enough. You must want it with
an inner exuberance that erupts through the
skin and joins the energy that created the
world.*

Sheilah Graham

Recurring fantasies of unattainable dreams may
have become pockets of pleasure for our down times.
A faraway place or person, images of home, past
moments of glory—perhaps we have considered them
lost forever.

Dare we try to make a fragment of one of these
wishes come true? Of course we can! If we believe
middle age is an impediment, we are using the greatest
cop-out of all. We are capable of more than we have
ever imagined.

We may need to mobilize ourselves in a forgotten
direction to find the tangible goal of our fantasy. Hard
work, determination, self-discipline, patience, persist-
ence—we will need these real-world qualities and attitudes to make the fantasy real. At mid-life, however,
we have all these necessary ingredients, and we can
regain the self-confidence necessary to succeed.

*Today, let me choose a fantasy or an unfulfilled dream
and plot out how to bring it to fruition.*

November 1

The crucial task of old age is balance:
keeping just well enough, just brave enough,
just gay and interested and starkly honest
enough to remain a sentient human being.

Florida Scott-Maxwell

Have the unpleasant myths of old age prejudiced us against our own future? Now is the time to rethink these myths, reexamine our notions on old age, and take action. Our health, our bodies, our minds, our spirits, our friendships, our extended families, our activities, our goals, and our attitudes may all need an overhaul to enable us to move vitally into the years ahead.

Senility or helplessness are not inevitable. We are blessed to be in mid-life now, with time to make needed changes. We are capable of change; all the tools for making personal adjustments are at our disposal. As we age, we become role models for the next generation. We can show them the beauty of our 70s and 80s.

Today, let me begin to prepare for a bountiful and rewarding old age.

*People have the capacity to go either way—
toward growth or toward stagnation.*

           Chris Argyris

    We may feel flat, sluggish, and muddled for long stretches—days, weeks, sometimes months. Nothing clicks; our best efforts fall short. We are ill at ease. These feelings are not uncommon at mid-life. They may be residue from an illness, or a delayed reaction to stress. Or they may be seasonal, at the end of winter.

    We can learn to endure fallow times without panic; we can hang on and wait them out. Much is beyond our control. Nature remains mysterious. We can continue to do whatever is before us, knowing that "this too shall pass." Patience comes easier when we regain hope that this phase will end.

    Experience has taught us that these periods are often precursors to a new spurt of internal growth and vigor. We can look to nature as a model: the seasons follow one another with regularity; we trust their rhythms. So, too, can we trust our own. We will flower again.

Today, let me remember that I will be renewed, as I always have, if I maintain faith.

November 3

I'm a born-and raised Southerner, so I know something about conniption fits. You don't want to be around someone having a conniption fit; it's most unpleasant.

William Neikirk

Do we think "if only" in response to every problem of middle age? Do we wear ourselves and others down with constant complaints? Do we rage at life's unfairness when things get out of control or don't go our way?

Perhaps we have abdicated responsibility for our lives. Some of us may feel nothing but misery and frustration. We fear we are rapidly growing old, that we have lost control and thus hope.

Deep within us is a reservoir of strength and talents that can turn around our feelings of defeat and disappointment. We are inventive, resourceful, adaptive, and flexible. We've drawn on this reservoir before. It's how we survived. We can draw on it again.

Constructive solutions will come, one by one, as we begin to see ourselves as capable of handling anything that might come to us (which includes asking for help when we need it). One positive action lays the groundwork for the next. Block by block we build.

Today, let me turn away from complaining and believe in my life.

*Don't be afraid to occasionally yell and
scream. Not on a daily basis or anything,
but exercise your vocal cords from time to
time. It's good for you and won't hurt the
marriage. Don't get vicious, just loud.*

Randy Darling

Clear air is easy to breathe. A foggy atmosphere
promotes confusion, limited vision, heaviness. Sometimes clearing the air in a closed relationship can only
be done with a little yelling and screaming. It's the
only way to break the hold of our polite distance or
avoidance. Carefully choosing the words to get our
message across does not always work. Our partner
does not hear us.

If we find ourselves yelling, it is usually instinctive. We may have come to the end of our rope. Our
frustration is apparent and we are simply fed up. The
other person can hear us now. If, however, loudness is
the only way we know to be heard or to get our way, it
is probably counterproductive.

If we are willing to examine our intentions and
desires, and remember to let go and let God, we can
trust that a fair fight now and then can restore clarity
and directness to our relationship.

*Today, give me the courage to be forthright when it is
important to me.*

November 5

Of course, it is natural to care for our parents; we are flesh of their flesh after all. So we care for them as tenderly and with as good grace as we can.

Richard Atcheson

None of us is prepared for the role reversal that happens as our parents become infirm and aged. They may be forgetful and frail, ornery, stubborn, difficult, and demanding.

The obligation we may feel to look after the needs of our elderly parents can be terribly painful and unpleasant. The lurking implication is that we are also getting on in years. We may still yearn for our parents to be competent and capable of caring for us indefinitely, so we shy away from making major decisions about their long-range care, even though we know we must make them soon.

When we come to accept their helplessness and see the rewards inherent in our caring for them, we have reached another milestone. We have become the adults, at least! The assignment may have been thrust on us before we were ready for it, but it can bring out strengths we didn't know we had. We can grow into it. We can get more insight into what it means to be a son or a daughter.

Caring for our aging parents, and learning to set limits, can be a way of caring for ourselves. In coming to know them as they age we come to know ourselves.

Today, let me approach my parents' care with care for myself.

Tis grace that brought me safe thus far.
Tis grace will lead me home.

> *John Newton ("Amazing*
> *Grace")*

Grace is of music and the wind, invisible to my eye.

Grace is of my heart and soul, my guardian, first and last friend, celebrator of my spirit.

Grace is hard to understand when I demand to touch and see.

It is the answer in between the lines. Intuition opens the door to readiness. Sometimes doesn't a special coincidence happen at just the right time?

When I am utterly exhausted, grace keeps me in the game.

We say that we don't deserve grace, or need any special favors. Why is it so hard for us to accept a gift. we didn't "earn?"

That is exactly why we are given grace: because we believe that we aren't "good" enough.

Today, let me feel that grace is my Higher Power's visibly invisible proof of love, protection, and the knowledge that we are good enough.

November 7

Anger is usually the flipside of helplessness.
Eliana Gil

Sustained anger can erode our insides and keep us trapped in pain and frustration. Anger that gets no relief, that cannot find a resolution, may be a signal that we are feeling powerless. Rather than hounding the object of our anger we may need to look at the limits of our power. Admitting our powerlessness is the first step to getting some power back.

Hurt by a neighbor's sarcastic comment we may be angry because we didn't immediately react. Maybe we're frustrated and angry at our powerlessness to direct our children along the path we think would be "good for them." Work, when it isn't going our way, can make us feel angry, powerless, and ineffective.

We all need to feel our personal power. Trapped in anger, we may not realize that we are really reacting to feelings of helplessness and loss of control. Anger can point to those feelings that we wouldn't see without it. Identifying and accepting our powerlessness can ease our frustration enough so we can step back and take stock of the real problem. With distance we can ask for help in solving it. We can find a way out of the anger maze.

Today, let me take a closer look at my anger and feelings of powerlessness. Give me the courage to grieve my losses so I can move on.

*The constant emphasis upon her physical
appearance, is in truth, a very hard rap for
a woman to beat.*

  Maggie Scarf

It has been suggested that a man's greatest mid-
life fear is of death and that a woman's is of aging.
Because our culture defines women by their appearance, for many women the natural occurrence of wrinkles and sags feels like the beginning of the end.

Some of us worry about who will like us when our
bodies and faces change. Will we even be able to like
ourselves? Coming to terms with our aging bodies is a
mid-life task. If we've been taught to define ourselves
in terms of traditional standards of youthful beauty we
may not be challenged to rethink years of propaganda
and youth-cult conditioning.

We can take our power back. It's up to us, not
advertisers, to define beauty and attractiveness. Wrinkles look different when we are seeing them through
our own eyes. When our definition of beauty is
informed by self-acceptance we will have gone a long
way toward healing ourselves and toward allaying a
great fear that controls so many of us.

*Today, let me feel the power and energy that come
from accepting and valuing myself as I am in this
moment.*

November 9

Dios quiere—"God wills it." In Spanish, it also means, "God loves it."

John Dunne

It is difficult to believe that when God brings us pain, God is also bringing us love. If we were to stand on a high hill and look back over the days of our lives, we could see the seeds of God's love in the green and brown landscape. Where once we could see only tragedy we may now see blessing.

As we come to know that God's will for us is good and loving, we gain serenity. In plumbing the depths of our own lives we learn of the depth of God's absolute love for us. Even in our darkest moments, we can trust God will not desert us.

God has given us special graces to enable us to sail into the windstorms of our lives. Gradually we can learn how to relax and ride God's wings of grace. In doing so we may find that the less we struggle the more we are able to surrender ourselves to trust.

We can trust that our God is friendly and on our side. Though we may not understand God's direction, it is safe to let go and ride the current.

Today, let me trust God's will for me.

Nothing hurts more than being ignored.
        Sam Friend

Indifference is one of the worst kinds of punishment. It wounds by ignoring if not outright denying the existence of the other person. Indifference may say to them, "You don't count enough to deserve a response from me." Indifference is the opposite of forgiveness and letting go.

Are there people in our lives who have done such bad things that they deserved to be discounted? Indifference reflects unfinished business. When we deliberately ignore someone we may still be connected by the live energy of our anger.

It takes courage to honestly inventory and then be willing to let go of our resentments. Then we are free to choose how to best take care of ourselves in the relationship without the bond of cold indifference. We are truly free in our relationships only when we have the courage to let go of our punishing behaviors.

Today, help me see if I am chained to anyone by angry indifference.

November 11

My wife and I tried to have breakfast together but we had to stop or my marriage would have been wrecked.

Winston Churchill

Sometimes our shared time may turn into an interrogation: Have you done this? When will you fix the window? We need information, but we don't need to overbear or control to get it.

Our attitude can set the stage for either harmony or discord. Nothing shuts down communication quicker than little digs, angry gestures, or demanding comments. When we let go of our angry edge at the talk table both parties benefit. Expressing anger without shaming or attacking won't put the other person on the defensive. Resolution is far more likely when we're both safe from personal attack.

After a hurtful comment, one husband gently asked his wife, "Is that a happy question?" His question made her rephrase hers. Taking a few deep breaths and pausing to think of the kindest ways to communicate takes a lot of the pain out of talk.

Today, let me look at how I communicate in my marriage and relationships. Let me direct without attacking.

*It seems to me you lived your life like a
candle in the wind. Never knowing who
to cling to when the rains set in.*

   Elton John

Some of us have a hard time letting others comfort
us when we're hurting. We feel vulnerable, like we've
lost control. Early on, we learned the caretaker's
creed: You will be loved only if you care for others;
people leave you when you depend on them. Caring
becomes caretaking when we routinely neglect our
own needs to give to others. When we neglect ourselves we lose balance. We may grow to resent the
people, places, and things that we give to.

To receive from others, we first need to stop, take
a breath, and figure out what we need. It is a measure
of how much we love when we can ask someone to
care for us. When we realize that we do need others,
we will have come a long way toward loving ourselves
and them.

*Today, let me trust someone enough to tell him or her
what I need.*

November 13

*Grandmother grows in dignity as the fall
turns towards winter.*

Sharon R. Curtin

There is an old Japanese story about a grandmother who decides it is her winter to go out to the mountain and die. She quietly prepares for the journey. Her family is grown and they all know she is preparing for death as she cleans her house one final time. She spends her last days with her children and grandchildren, leaving her imprint on their hearts for all time. Having completed her preparations, she sits and waits for the snow.

When we view death as a part of life, it becomes more a friend than an enemy. All of life has its time and its season, a time to live and a time to die. Nature can teach us about this ebb and flow. In nature, death is as purposeful, as interwoven in the order of things, as life. It is also, like life, a transition. To live fully in this moment is the finest preparation we can bring to our own season of transition.

Today, let me not fear death. Let me believe that death is a natural transition and part of life.

Man is born with rainbows in his heart.
        Carl Sandburg

We all have the capacity for joy. In spite of our pains, woes, and troubles, joy is waiting to be welcomed back home. Balance is what can usher it in. When more than one area of our lives is consistently out of balance, our ability to feel joy may be diminished. When we are at peace, we sow the soil that joy grows best in.

Joy can be found in the most common places, moments, and activities. A patch of sunlight on the carpet, the sway and wind call of tall trees, the round curve of a child's brown belly in a pile of sand. Joy may be soaring or calm, but it always affirms a rightness. We know we are exactly in the right place at this moment in time.

Joy belongs to us today. We are all worthy of joy's presence. The more we see the world through the eyes of our internal child, the wider will be our capacity for joy at its most commonplace.

Today, let me be open to the simple treasures all around me in life and nature.

November 15

Love yourself as your neighbor.
                        Frederick Buechner

Real love of ourselves and others grows out of self-acceptance. We are often our own worst critics. Many of us set impossibly high standards and then spend all our available energy being mad at ourselves for not meeting them. We may ask ourselves: Why don't you exercise more? Why don't you have a better prayer and meditation life? Why don't you have deeper friendships and healthier relationships? Why don't you make more money? The more we struggle with our supposed shortcomings, the more tired and farther from positive change we seem to get.

Stuck between a rock and a dozen hard places, we can find relief if we are willing to lighten up and get off our own cases. Accepting ourselves today and acknowledging that we are exactly where we are supposed to be is the beginning of health and change. Self-criticism produces negative energy and depression. Instead of faultfinding, we can choose to begin "gift finding." Every day we can focus on one good thing about ourselves.

Self-acceptance heals our shame and frees up our energy such that we can make changes in our lives. The sun shines brighter when we resign from the habit of self-blame and give God room to work in our day.

Today, let me be conscious of how I blame myself so that I can begin to heal.

*God's way may be harder for you but it will
be easier on you.*

H. Hanson

If the first forty years of our lives seemed like a
ride on a speeding locomotive the last forty may look
like a lesson in how to apply the brakes. Decreasing
energy and increasing introspection bring us face to
face with the greatest challenge of all. How do we stop
living on the fast track when the fast track is second
nature?

Until recently, our lives may have been focused on
accomplishments and caring for others. But those we
once cared for may now be independent. Many of our
goals have in fact been realized. Still we keep up the
frantic pace, though it zaps our energy. Many of
us, however, are now asking in response, Is this all
there is?

Wanting a different life and making it happen is
challenging mid-life work. Most of us find it hard to let
go of our old life. We hold on to our fast pace as if it
were a rock in a river. Beaten black and blue by life's
currents, we still hold tight.

We can trust that when we let go of that rock we'll
be carried down to a more serene bend in the river.
Most of our pain is not in change but in our resistance
to change.

*Today, let me release my old habits and attitudes trust-
ing that I will be guided in a good direction.*

November 17

*Take the time to look in your heart and be
clear. Walk through life being clear. Practice
doing each thing in peace.*

Hugh Prather

A fearful unsettled mind can quickly ruin our day.
Our emotional condition is more important to our
well-being than how we dress or have our hair styled.
When our thinking is frantic and jumbled, we easily
get separated from life's moment-by-moment vitality.

Worries about money, work, health, and children
can run rampant if we give them the green light.
There is always something to worry about, yet most of
us have already forgotten what we were so stressed out
about last week. On most days life takes care of itself if
we let it.

Many of us believe that if we worry enough it will
affect any given situation for the better. Chronic worry
can be changed if we are willing to look at what is generating it. Who would we be or what would we be
doing if we weren't worrying? What beliefs keep us
feeling afraid and insecure? Do we still believe them?
What are we willing to change? Maybe worrying is not
necessary. The joy of going to sleep at night with peace
of mind and waking up free of dread is ample reward
for plowing up and exposing our garden of worry.

*Today, let me get honest with myself and another per-
son about the deeper feelings that are generating my
anxiety and worry.*

*Is your love of God secure enough that you
can rage against Him?*

Anthony de Mello

Sometimes we get mad at God. We may feel that
we can't bear what is happening in our lives. Does our
God have wide enough shoulders to accept both our
anger and our love? We can trust God with our negative and our positive feelings the same as we would a
good friend who we share our deepest selves with. Perhaps giving our God all of our feelings is the ultimate
form of trust and love. Pouring out our deepest feelings
may say to God, "I trust you enough to be the real
human being you created."

If expression is healing, to believe that God can
bear our deepest rage and confusion is the beginning
of healing. Feeling safe enough to express these feelings to another person often follows. Thus does healing happen.

To share with God all that is inside our hearts
instantly lightens our burden. So lightened we trust
further. And we grow.

*Today, let me trust in God's unconditional love and
understanding of my best and worst.*

November 19

Yelling at living things does tend to kill the spirit in them. Sticks and stones may break our bones, but words will break our hearts.

Robert Fulghum

Loving others brings with it a responsibility to be kind. We all have days in which we feel stretched to our limit. Days in which everyone seems not to get us. The car has a new rattle, our boss isn't smiling, and our checkbook didn't balance. Short-fuse days seem to dry up our tolerance until we feel that we deserve to dump our frustration on the next person who crosses our path. The people we love the most often bear the brunt of our anger.

Yelling, shouting, or being sarcastic with others doesn't relieve stress but makes more stress. Words that hurt—verbal attacks and accusations—are weapons of sadness and pain.

Today we can choose to take responsibility for our problems instead of exploding. We can write, talk, pray, and walk away our frustrations instead of hurling them at others.

It feels great to look at ourselves in the mirror at the end of a day in which we didn't hurt anyone with our words.

Today, let me guard and take responsibility for my words. Before I say anything, let me ask myself: Is it kind?

*Bagels, sun, coffee, a friend . . . and then
some solitude are the flowers of my morning.*

Samuel Cohen

Maturity may be found in acknowledging our spiritual hungers and our need to feed them. As we stop yearning for an abundance of things we may get acquainted with our true selves. As we let go of our internal clutter and clatter, we are better able to sit still within our own silence.

Discovering and fulfilling our spiritual needs may feel lonely at times. Letting go of our old rushing ways, initially creates a void. But the fact that we're willing to do so says we're equal to the challenge of moving through our fear of aloneness into the healing grace of solitude.

Solitude can taste like sun, air, and water to our thirsty spirits. Once we have tasted the healing that accompanies solitude, we crave its return. Solitude refuels us. It enables us to greet the day and everything it brings. To guard our times of solitude is to nourish ourselves.

Today, let me value and protect my solitude.

November 21

*Look back upon your life . . . the moments
that stand out . . . are the moments when
you have done things in the spirit of love.*

Henry Drummond

Making peace with our children can be an important part of our life work. Worrying about how our children turn out is useless. They will turn out exactly like us. Our character defects are often mirrored in our children and nothing makes us madder. If we have not looked at ourselves, however, we may not recognize these similarities. What three things anger us most about a particular child? How are we the same?

Learning to be patient with our own shortcomings can give us more patience with and understanding of our children. Judging ourselves and those we love harshly wears us out long before the day is done. How will we be today? Will we choose to be basically friendly or basically critical in our interactions with our children?

Working on our own shortcomings leads us to tolerate and accept them in others. When we can forgive ourselves we can forgive our children.

Today, let me decide if I want to spend another day angry at my child.

As for old age, embrace and love it. It
abounds with pleasure, if you know how
to use it.

> *Seneca*

A prerequisite for enjoying life is the belief that we deserve to be happy. There was a man named Ralph who believed happiness was an accident. If the cards of life feel right, you might get a few moments of joy, now and then. Ralph never learned how to sing or play or celebrate life. He was almost surprised to catch himself feeling happy. He didn't believe he deserved happiness or pleasure, so the older he got the more somber he became. Eventually he was spending most of his days in front of the TV wondering what else to do to pass the time. Ralph was not prepared for the joys of age.

It is never too late to open up to life. Each morning gives us an opportunity to try on a new piece of living. We are never doomed to gloom and despair. What a thrill to sign up for Yoga, become a volunteer, or meet a good friend for lunch. We can actively reprogram ourselves each morning to reach out instead of isolating.

Today, let me practice expecting to be happy as I get older. Help me reach out to others.

November 23

To remain silent when we love someone is heartbreaking

        James Robertson

Who are the last people we would what to see before we close our eyes and die? Whatever picture comes to mind is the picture we have been given to cherish while we are alive. Many of us see the faces of loved ones and family members. What an opportunity we have to love those people today! Are we holding resentments or bitterness in our hearts? Do the people we love know how much they mean to us? Have we told them today?

Many of us rarely tell the people closest to us how we feel about them. We rationalize that they already know how we feel about them. The harder it is for us to say "I love you" the more we need to say it. And the more our special others need to hear it.

Today is our opportunity to risk, open up, and share our hearts with those we care about.

Today, let me believe that my love is worthy enough to be shared with others.

*To be "whole" at the same time means to be
full of contradictions.*

            Jolande Jacobi

Today it is okay for us to give our imperfect gifts. Everything we do counts, whether half or full measure. On some days we can give life our best efforts but on others we are lucky just to make it through. On those days the only thing that counts is our willingness to just "show up." If we expect perfection of ourselves, we will regularly be disappointed.

Perfectionism can wear us out, not to mention whoever happens to be in the way on our road to "getting life right." Is life a journey to be lived and enjoyed or a task to be completed? Maybe the most rewarding days are those during which we relax and give ourselves a little slack. Learning to say "easy does it" and "lighten up" can help chase the monkey of perfectionism off our backs.

Today, let me relax and realize I don't have to be perfect.

November 25

I often turn in a crowded city to stare at a face on which experience has written a pattern of celebration.

Mary Francis Shura Craig

Life and how we live it is written on our faces. We have all known people who remain positive through everything. We can be that person who celebrates rather than mourns life. It feels wonderful to be around a life celebrator. In a room full of people, we are drawn to that person whose eyes, and laughter welcome us without judgment.

Negativity and judging ourselves and others induces frown lines and wrinkles faster than any July sun. What type of person do we choose to be? We can learn to relax a little and let go of negative thinking.

Tolerance and openness act as magnets. People flock to us when we are open to whatever or whoever they bring. It is never too late to put on a happy face and begin the day with a forgiving and joy-filled heart.

Today, let me remember that joy is contagious. When I give away joy, I catch it myself.

Adults are children too, because in every adult heart there is a child's life that will stay there for eternity. So please listen to children. Because when you don't, it is like not listening to yourself.

    Lalita Riggs

Children always seem to pop into our days. When our own children are adults, we visit with our grandchildren or the boy or girl next door. Growing older, we may have less energy but hopefully more patience and wisdom with little ones. Age can thaw out our hearts, make us more sensitive to the tug of a small hand in ours. We may have made mistakes with children before, but opportunity does knock twice.

To listen well to a child is a gift of immeasurable value. It is to know, finally, that listening, not lecturing, is the heart of love. So now we can sit in the grass or in the bleachers of a Little League park and laugh with and listen to the children who find their way into our lives.

To make time for the children in our lives is to make time for the child in us. It is true that they keep us young.

Today, let me listen to a child.

November 27

*Don't worry about opposition. Remember a
kite rises against the wind, not with the
wind.*

Hamilton Wright Mabie

Were we to be described in three words at our
death, what would we have the words be? We can write
our own epitaph. We can choose how we will live out
the rest of our days. Those three words can challenge
us to determine what thoughts, actions, and attitudes
would create the person we want to be.

We may have to let go of old behaviors and reactions to accomplish our goals. But willingness to
change and grow is the first step. Old negative behaviors are hard to let go of. Waking up grouchy in the
morning may have guaranteed that we wouldn't be
disturbed before our morning coffee. Sitting in an
easy chair still may seem a lot easier than taking the
walk the doctor ordered. To get what we want, however, we need to give up what has stopped working
for us. We may find ourselves so delighted with the
results that we wonder why we struggled so long with
letting go.

Today, let me paint my own life portrait.

*It seems that most folks most of the time
simply get through life. Their days are spent
merely passing time until the weekends or
until their vacations.*

   David K. Reynolds

Planning for and worrying about the future or
obsessing on the past robs us of today. Intellectually,
we know all we have is now, yet we may still spend a
majority of our time chained to the past and future.

We're driving to get a haircut. But we're not
there. We're worrying about starting dinner on time or
paying the electric bill. How much actual living do we
lose as thoughts whirl around in our heads? The reality of our drive becomes lost in another dimension.

What if we were to stop and focus our attention on
the present moment? Maybe we would meet our real
selves. Maybe we would feel the sun on our necks,
hear the hum and rattle of the car, feel and know our
living feelings.

For many of us, all too used to zigzagging
between past and future, being present can be quite a
challenge. The challenge is to be with ourselves and
thus alive in a way we cannot be when we are living in
our thoughts about the past or future. In the present is
where we come to know ourselves, and others.

*Today, help me bring my attention back to the moment
whenever I find myself worrying or preoccupied.*

November 29

*Years may wrinkle the skin but to give up
interest wrinkles the soul.*

Douglas MacArthur

Life gives us as much adventure as our vision will
allow. We can accomplish only what we are willing to
dream. We are as limited as our fears.

With many of our structured years behind us, we
now have the opportunity to reshape our destiny. Many
of us begin planning for retirement and adventure in
our 30s, 40s, and 50s. Instead of being put out to pasture, we are choosing to create our own field of
dreams, to make our own spiritual and emotional
fortunes.

We can choose how we will live our last fifty
years. Daring to plan early on can make our dreams
come true. It is never too early to risk living as we
really want to live.

Are we cutting back on nonessential tasks or are
we taking on more and more limiting responsibilities?
We must make the space in our lives so our dreams can
grow and develop. Today is when we can start planning for our future. What risks are we willing to take?
What changes are we willing to make so our lives can
be the way we want them to be? When will we begin?

*Today, let me believe that I deserve to have my dreams
come true. Let me do one thing to make them happen.*

The essence of genius is to know what to overlook.

William James

Our days are full of "overlook" opportunities. One key to serenity is knowing what to overlook and let go of. Maybe a co-worker makes a mistake that doesn't directly affect us. Maybe the dinner we're served is cold, but it's served with love. Maybe the toothpaste has been squeezed from the top instead of the bottom, again; or our teenager's made a smart remark. Maybe we've made a mistake. We can choose to overlook these things, to direct our attention to the solution instead of the difficulty.

Overlooking doesn't mean that we approve of a situation. It means only that we are choosing not to make it a big deal. Power flows into our life when we learn to observe without reacting negatively.

As we come to trust our intuition, we become better able to judge the seriousness of a situation and to respond accordingly. Serenity is a precious treasure that we retain by learning what is and isn't our concern today.

Today, help me overlook the minor inconveniences and small irritations of daily living.

December 1

*I wish you songs but also blessed silence
and God's sweet peace when every day
is done.*

Dorothy Nell McDonald

Many of us see peace as a luxury; others see it as a necessity. Life is teaching many of us, however, to get back to basics. Maybe wealth, fame, or status no longer warm us at the end of the day. Not like peace does—whether of mind or in our homes or relationships.

We can make peace a daily priority. We can learn to avoid stressful people, places, and things. Nothing is worth the loss of our serenity and peace of mind.

Limit setting and time management may take on a new meaning in our quest for peace. Setting goals and planning ahead can eliminate unnecessary stress and friction in every arena of our lives.

We don't come to value peace by accident. It usually results from having been around the block more than once. That trip's great lesson is that there is nothing more essential than peace. Without the harmony and balance it breeds, nothing of value can grow.

Today, let me find peace. Help me let go of the people, places, and situations that rob me of serenity.

*The best part about this fight is we can both
come out of it winners.*

K.J. LaFlam

A fight with loved ones may bring out the best and
the worst in us. The people who love us most are also
the most vulnerable in our presence and therefore the
most easily hurt. How can we balance our need to
express our anger and frustration with our desire to
love with gentleness and responsibility?

Love at its best seeks to build others up. It would
respect at all costs rather than attack the soft under-
belly exposed to us in trust. There need be no contradiction between loving well and fighting well if we are
willing to express our feelings without attacking or
belittling the other person. A good fight need last no
longer than five minutes. Ideally it ought to stay in the
now and end with a few minutes of quiet time and a
mutual commitment to move on to a neutral topic.

It is healing to express our anger and frustration,
but not if we shame another person in the process.
When we take responsibility for our feelings and think
before we talk, we plant seeds for a mature, give-and-
take love to grow.

*Today, let me keep my mouth closed until I can speak
without shaming another person.*

December 3

*We come to love wounded . . . begin the
lost and endless pilgrimage toward becoming a lover in the middle of a junkyard of
broken myths, shattered relationships,
smashed illusions, tarnished heroes and
absolute gods.*

Sam Keen

When we are feeling most broken is often when
we discover the soul mate of our life. We may be given
the gift of love's absolution when we feel we least
deserve it. Doubting our ability to successfully love
and be loved we are challenged to trust again.

We may have traveled many emotional miles and
experienced deep hurts so that we might now appreciate the opportunity love brings us. Tempered with
pain, we may find that we no longer take love's grace
for granted. Gratitude may be at the heart of our later
life love experience.

Age can renew our respect and appreciation for
the miracle of love. We may now find that love blooms
abundantly when we nurture it with gratitude.

What small thing can we do for our loved one
today? With God's help we can build a mountain of
gratitude in our lives.

*Today, let me rejoice and be grateful for the possibility
of loving at any age.*

God loves us the way we are, but He loves us too much to leave us that way.

Leighton Ford

God is a great challenger, letting us get into all types of jams only to challenge us to grow and risk. There always seems to be a new risk to take as we open the door on God's day. We may find ourselves daring a new task, dream, or behavior that we thought impossible a year ago. Our fears can seem like God's bowling pins—standing up only to get knocked down.

Growth is scarey as well as challenging. We may wonder if the new limb we're about to step out on will hold our weight. Yet we keep stepping out, perhaps because we trust that if we do fall we will be cushioned by God's grace.

Some days we may wonder where God's vision and plan will take us. Perhaps the destination isn't as important as people, places, and moments we encounter along the way.

Each of us has a blueprint of wonders in our hands that is exactly right for where we are right this moment. Sometimes we may wish to just sit back and marvel at what God has in store for us around the bend.

Today, let me be aware of God's active work in my life.

December 5

Communication between the generations is reversed; parents can and must learn from their children, who are more at home in the present world than the parents are.

Theodore M. Hesburgh

Openmindedness, interest, attention, and appreciation—can we give these gifts to our now-grown children? We may feel humble yet proud to admit that our sons and daughters are becoming worthwhile human beings in their own right. Humble because they evince many of the values we've transmitted; proud that our years of difficult and persistent parenting have yielded these fine young adults.

As they establish their independence from us, former roles are blurred. We are challenged to stay open to them, to keep our "I know better" attitude.

We can learn to see them as unique individuals. Dare we become friends with one another? By encouraging their growth away from us and applauding their specialness, awe can build a new relationship. Their fresh approach and intense involvement with the world of today can astound us. We can learn from them.

Today, let me listen to my child and hear an adult.

*I have been driven many times to my knees
by the overwhelming conviction that I had
nowhere else to go.*

Abraham Lincoln

Loved children naturally trust and go to the parents for help. Within each of us still lives the little child who needs help. What a relief to accept that we don't have to have all the answers. Prayer and meditation can help us let go of believing we must have all the answers. They can lead us to the answers and solutions that come from outside ourselves. Our prayer life is the one time each day when we can safely reveal every part of ourselves—the good, the weak, the doubtful, the fearful. When we pray we lower our blood pressure. We open ourselves to trusting that we are always being perfectly cared for in all situations. Problems that baffle and confuse us can be given to our God for direction and guidance.

What a relief when we accept that we are not alone in our worries, fears, and joys. Praying daily is a habit that can be cultivated like flowers that need only the simplest care and attention in order to flourish.

Today, let me trust anew that God is absolutely there to care for me.

December 7

*The keys to the Kingdom of Heaven are
found in the respective ways we treat others
in relationships.*

Kate Tobin

Marriage and committed relationships are the laboratory in which we learn that life is not a fairy tale. Amid pain, joy, and passions, we learn of our essential aloneness. No one else is responsible for making us happy. We are powerless to change another human being.

Good marriages and relationships don't seem good all of the time. And when they are good it's because both people have worked at it. We can learn at first to tolerate and later to respect if not cherish our differences. Even still, many a disagreement will never feel settled until both partners feel they have won. Then comes the next lesson. It is just as important to know when to be quiet and not react as to know when to talk. Most difficulties are negotiable if we approach them with a loving non-attack attitude.

When there is a foundation of mutual respect for differences, love deepens.

Today, let me get honest about what I can begin to change about my relationship, reactions, and attitudes.

We are all made of star stuff.
Carl Sagan

We are all eternally interwoven with the universe. The calcium in our teeth, the iron in our blood, and the carbon in our applesauce originally composed the interior of a star. Men and women alike are connected to our planet home through the mysteries of birth, death, and renewal. So do we and the earth endure. It is our privilege and responsibility to conserve its resources and protect its inhabitants.

As we age, our connection to earth grows stronger. Walking along a shoreline, climbing a mountain, crossing a field, we may feel parental in our desire to care for the land. We may come to understand that we do not own it, that at best we are its custodians, holding it in trust for our children's children. God speaks best to us outdoors. We may dream of the day when, holding a child's hand, we can walk in a place we love, sharing its magic and telling its tale.

Today, let me do one thing to preserve and cherish our planet.

December 9

*Taking joy in life is a woman's best
cosmetic.*

Rosalind Russell

Today, we may be trying to come to terms with
our appearance. We may be fighting off age when the
real enemy lies elsewhere. Feeling desperate to change
the way we look can reflect internal distress.

Before we do something drastic like cosmetic sur-
gery we need to examine our expectations. Correcting
what we perceive to be a facial or bodily flaw can
indeed change our self-image, boost our self-
confidence. But changing the surface won't change us
if we don't change. Soon enough they'll be something
else in the mirror that will make us want to throw
darts. We will still age.

Moderate exercise, a healthy diet, attention to
grooming—not to mention attention to our emotional
and spiritual selves—these things connote a self-
respect that cannot be purchased or patched on. It is a
self-respect—and a beauty—that can be seen by those
who would see.

Today, let my appearance and manner reflect me.

For five days I worked on brightening my attitude and much to my amazement, my life greatly improved for the better.

    William Pugh

"Lighten Up" is a helpful slogan to remember on our too-serious days. In the light of eternity, what is really important? At times we may become so caught up in our thoughts and actions that we forget the impact we have on others.

Chronic seriousness can be deadly. It may erode our good nature and considerably dampen the spirits of our companions and loved ones. Some days we may take ourselves so seriously that a gray cloud of negative energy follows us from room to room. Rushing, worrying, complaining, and pushing wear us and others out.

We can choose what emotional hat we'll put on this morning. What color will it be today? What kind of attitude and image? We are the master of our attitude and emotional outlook. It is never too late to begin a good day.

Today, let me be aware of the effect my attitude has on myself and others.

December 11

*Even if I knew that tomorrow the world
would go to pieces, I would still plant my
own apple tree.*

Martin Luther

We are our own destination. This life is a voyage
to an island of peace and solitude deep within ourselves. Along the way we meet life's monsters, many
of whom at first appear to have beautiful faces. We get
sidetracked, lulled into the false belief that peace can
be discovered outside ourselves. The perfect romance,
drink, drug, food, dress—just the right amount of
exercise or work—we pursue these things as if they
could satisfy us, as if they could fix all our problems.

They turn out to lead nowhere. In the end, they
are empty and we are alone. Pain and grief enable us to
be open to the grace of God. We can learn that the
answers and safety we seek lie within. When pain and
loss throw us back on ourselves, we are thrown back
finally upon our own power to heal. We can choose to
accept our limitations. We can choose to love ourselves in our fragility. When we do so we may find that
we are not alone, that we have never been.

*Today, let me welcome my journey into myself guided
by God's love and faith in me.*

Live with the past not in it.
Teri Sue Livingston

Making friends with our past is an act of self-love and forgiveness. Staying stuck in regret, loss, and past pain is like robbery. We rob today when we are unwilling to make peace with the past. Our past is one of our best teachers. None of us steps out of yesterday a saint or superhuman. We walk into today stamped as a human being.

Yesterday is a reality, but when it continues to control our lives it can become a tyrant. Constant reviewing and lamenting can keep us sick, depressed, and poor company for our family and friends.

Today, is all we have. We can grieve our losses and make peace with yesterday or we can hold on, blind to the possibilities of today. Moments fully lived are like jewels that never lose their luster. When we practice staying in the now, we get to meet our real selves face to face. Nothing makes us feel more alive than being present in the minutes and seconds of today.

Today, let me release the pain of yesterday. Let me bring the lessons of the past into today.

December 13

To listen to another person with total atten-
tion and patience, to listen with no attempts
to interrupt, to listen with no condemning
judgment, is what unconditional love is
all about.

Gerald G. Jampolsky

We may think that unconditional love is a tall order reserved only for saints. Unconditional love sounds complicated and unreachable to our time-worn hearts. What a surprise it is to find out that we all have the capacity to love others without judgment and control. Unconditional love is simply our ability to sit with another person and truly be there for them. When we love unconditionally, we come with empty out-stretched hands. We then offer our hands, inviting the other to fill them up. We can only begin to do this when we have already met our own needs. This way we don't come looking for a handout for ourselves, or with an agenda of our own for the other person. We are simply there for the other person to use for support, without judgment or shame.

What a privilege to sit with another person and allow them to be who they really are. Nothing feels better than acceptance. Most people are their own worst judge and critic and, given time, they usually struggle through to their own solution. In the midst of our pain, what we all need most is just someone to be there with us without judging.

Today, let me believe that I can practice loving unconditionally.

I think that's the crucial test of love—
whether it generates new life in others

Daisy Newman

When love is life-giving it seems to envelope the people in our lives with warmth and good cheer. When love between two people is based on respect and honesty, there occurs a natural overflowing. We experience a sort of bubbling over of goodness and happy energy when we walk into a room where love is actively present.

We are continually challenged to choose between tolerance and fear when we love. Fear may cause us to respond to others with jealousy, control, and possessiveness. Practicing tolerance of the differences of others gives us the freedom to reach out and love them in spite of their faults or shortcomings.

Life-giving relationships are the ones in which we don't feel judged and criticized, but are accepted for our goodness and value. The more we give the gift of loving tolerance to others, the more it is contagiously returned.

Today, let me focus on loving others in spite of my fears and insecurities.

December 15

Life is half spent before we know what it is.
George Herbert

Hesitation is the enemy of creativity. Creative ideas come to us at the right and perfect times and action makes our dreams become reality. How often have we said, "What a great idea, I wish I would have thought of it."

All of us are capable of following through on great ideas if we learn to listen and respond to our intuitions. We may have been taught to hesitate and think things through too much to make sure we don't make a mistake.

New ideas, ventures, and creative activities are meant to be tried, mistakes and all. We find that correcting mistakes is part of the creative process. Fear of making mistakes will keep us stuck and leave us admiring the risks and creativity of others.

We can begin to trust and listen to the small voice that says, "That's a good idea for a song," or, "I have an idea about how my work department can increase productivity."

Our silence and hesitation will disappear as we practice risk-taking and listening to our creative intuition, and we will begin to take steps toward our full potential.

Today, I will start an ongoing list of all the good ideas that "pop into my head" and I will be willing to act on them regularly.

Loneliness is the pain of being alone;
solitude is the joy of being alone.

  Ralph Takach

Sometimes we walk a fine line between loneliness and solitude. We are lonely when our children or our spouses are gone or our friends seem too few or too busy. We are stuck with ourselves and are uncomfortable. We grope for a way to fill the emptiness.

In our middle years we can arrive at a juncture where we choose consciously to let go of this hurt, to prune it away. In its place we can be sure we will see new growth. Our inner resources can truly be trusted.

As we become centered with thoughts and feelings focused on today, our own company becomes sufficient. Much of our time in solitude is spent reflecting, integrating, doing personal work, creating.

Loneliness will re-emerge from time to time when our inner resources wane and need recharging. We can then seek the laughter of others to restore our smile. We can welcome chatter, questions, and even annoyances for the sake of interaction, and soon our balance is restored.

Today, let me offset my need for sociability with my need for drawing apart from others.

December 17

*Because of Anne-Marie I really know what
a birthday means now; a new life, the true
reason to celebrate.*

Marc Simon

The joy of birth is preceded by anxiety, pain,
trust, and hard work. The annual day commemorating
our birth may also be clouded by fears as we have
another reminder, in mid-life, how quickly our years
are fleeing.

What we do is learn not to cringe at the calendar.
We glance back over the past year, relieved it's over,
and congratulate ourselves on surviving its bumps and
shocks. We look forward, plan a bit, and wish secretly
for substantial good in the year ahead.

Opportunities will be there! Whether or not today
is our birthday, we can take a long look at ourselves,
and find, overall, it is good, we are good.

We welcome the sense of direction and renewal
this brings us, grateful to live in this period of history,
aware of our gifts and unique contributions we've
given to those around us. A sense of newness fills this
special day, and deep satisfaction.

*Today, let me rejoice in my own birth long ago and the
chance to live this day well.*

You shall have joy or you shall have power,
said God; you shall not have both.

Ralph Waldo Emerson

In African villages where Western ways have not yet intruded, the rhythm and pace is as unhurried today as it has been for hundreds of years. Being intimate with nature and depending on the land for survival brings a profound reverence and wisdom as well.

The Muslim influence, and its practice of praying five times each day, appears as a natural part of this uncomplicated lifestyle. The prayer-caller urges the villagers to stop and reflect on the great Being.

In our middle years we often try desperately to simplify our lives, to untangle the web we've spun for ourselves. We may feel helpless in the grip of a culture which thrives on stress, a ferocious work ethic, guilt feelings, and nameless dreads.

We need to step away from the mainstream. We must dig through layers of complexity to uncover a way of living that restores our authenticity. It may help to pray several times a day, and to begin to trust the Being Who transcends all religious practices.

Today, let me pray for simple peace of mind.

December 19

*How old would you be if you didn't know
how old you was?*

Satchel Paige

We grow up with a set of beliefs about aging. We remember what our parents were like at our age, and we see what they are like now. We have been deeply imprinted with the images and "duties" of middle age from the time we were children old enough to observe adults. How often now have we found ourselves acting a way we have learned through watching others? How often have we found ourselves saying the same things our parents said and laughing about it, or hating ourselves for it?

We are not those images from long ago. Those were other people, living in a different time, and those images were filtered through the lens of a child's perception. Our lives and our future life before us like an unbroken field of snow, and we can make any path we like on it. There is no obligation to do as we think we are expected to do. Nolan Ryan pitched a no hit game in the major leagues at the age of 43. No one had done this before, and most would have thought it impossible.

We are limited only by our own expectations, so let them at least be our own, and based on our abilities as we know them today. The more things we try, the more we will be surprised, and the fuller our lives will be.

Today, let me throw away one belief that limits my aspirations for tomorrow.

People living deeply have no fear of death.
        Anais Nin

Have we lived our lives in fear up to now? Have we not done things we wanted to do out of fear? Have we worried about trivial things, or shrunk back from adventures because we thought something else was "more important" at the time? What seems more important now?

We have only one life, and this is it. We are nearly halfway done with it, but we have learned the things that can help us do what we would once have thought was impossible. We have already been lucky to have lived this long. We have already been through enough fear and failure to know it can't really hurt us unless we allow it to. And if we risk all for something we want, what is the worst that can happen? Failure? Death? If we fail, we live to try again, and if we die, well, we'll all die anyway, so why not die living the way we want to live?

The world needs us, but it needs us to live on our terms, not out of fear but through our courage. When we take the time to look back and feel grateful for our lives so far; when we take stock of what's really important that's still to be done, then we are living deeply, and we are on a path of glory.

Today, let me take a step toward the life I've always wanted to live.

December 21

Unrest of spirit is a mark of life.
    Karl Menninger

After a move into a different environment, we expect a period of adjustment to the strangeness of new surroundings. This may be a time of comparing and complaining. At mid-life, however, we don't want to prolong this unease, so we settle in, accept what's here, and look for the good things this situation is offering us.

Our parents' rallying cry was: "Make do with what you have." That adage became, "Bloom where you are planted." When we ask ourselves if our cup is half empty or half filled, we know our response indicates optimism or pessimism in our perception.

Our attitude can make or break most situations. "It" and "They" do not have to change or vanish to insure our contentment, yet our own personal perspective may well need fine-tuning to resonate to the good surrounding us. When we decide to change our attitude, and only then, our half filled cup becomes full to overflowing!

Today, let me appreciate where I am without grumbling, then do one thing to improve my life.

It snowed and snowed the whole world over,
Snow swept the world from end to end. A
candle burned on the table, a candle
burned.

Boris Pasternak

Winter comes, taking a bite out of fall, leaving us all huddled and closer together. Winter is the time of patient waiting and silent growth.

The earth has its own deep-freeze business that keeps life resting until the spring thaw and the end of icy winds. Winter is the time we hibernate and pray for the storm to last one day longer. It is warm meals of chili, stew, and vegetable soup, and short days that seem married to the dark. It is romance and mystery, survival and contemplation, in front of a crackling fire.

Winter is a time for personal overhaul. Long nights give us time to reflect on our strengths and difficulties, our assets and liabilities. It is the time for new resolutions and new beginnings before the ground begins to soften and buds pop.

Winter is our maker of new beginnings and our season of ends. It is our time in between, to ready ourselves for April's misty mornings and daffodil miracles. If we use this time well, each spring will truly be a new beginning for us.

Today, let me find wonder and opportunity in the stern beauty of winter.

December 23

We learn geology the morning after the earthquake.

Ralph Waldo Emerson

It is so easy for us to feel stupid after making a mistake. We have felt the sting of failure or embarrassment often enough to know we don't like it and would love to avoid it from now on. Yet, time and again, we make mistakes. We may forget an appointment or do or say the wrong thing. We may put something together wrong, burn supper, drop a vase, or lock the keys in the car. Then, with all the hindsight that comes after the consequences arrive, we beat ourselves up for making mistakes.

But we're human, and we're learning. It's our nature to make mistakes and to learn from them. Most likely we're not making the same mistake over and over again. If we are, we have something profound to learn from that. And if we aren't, if we make new ones each time, then we're progressing. It's easy to feel like we're going nowhere when we feel that same old pain of failure, but we need to remember that the same old pain doesn't mean we're making the same old mistake. We can look at what we've done, learn from it, feel grateful to be better off than we were before, and move on. This way, we enjoy the victory embedded in every defeat.

Today, let me see the hidden treasure in my failures.

Even a fool, when he holdeth his peace, is counted wise.

Proverbs 17:28

It's so easy to offer needed advice when it isn't asked for. But as we remember the last time we did that, can we also remember what followed? Often an argument, hurt feelings, or anger is the outcome, and change is forgotten.

We can't change another, no matter how much good advice we offer. Like us, others must find their own way. If we are asked for advice, we also risk preaching, shaming, or controlling. We might say, "This is what I would do in your situation." Or we might say nothing, but continue to offer a listening ear. The best advice is often the silence in which the questioner can hear his or her own answers coming up from the heart. In this way we respect the other's wisdom, offer support without judgement, and participate in another's life without controlling or offending. Isn't this what we would want for ourselves?

Today, let me keep silent and simply listen to others.

December 25

The future you shall know when it has come; before then, forget it.

Aeschylus

It is so easy to forget what we need to do today by worrying about tomorrow. It is often the consequence of not doing what needs to be done today that we are so worried about. Other times, we worry about unknown disasters while a beautiful day for a picnic goes by unnoticed. When we do this, we are giving up our very lives.

Today, this moment, is all we have. We are only empowered to act in the present; we can only smell the flowers of the present; we can only laugh at today's jokes, not tomorrow's.

When we surrender tomorrow in order to live today more fully, we are enjoying our lives as they should be enjoyed. We are also giving ourselves the gift of a freer tomorrow, when we have given up control of the future, when we have acted as best we could on the day before, and when we have entered the present moment with our eyes on the life at hand.

Today, let me live in the present, and let the future take care of itself.

The unexamined life is not worth living.

>   *Socrates*

At some time or other we've all envied the person who never looks back, who never second-guesses himself, who never questions her own values or judgements or actions. We've wanted to be just like that person, to simply skate through life without a care or a regret. We may have thought of this as a way of living the simple life. It's not.

Living only on the surface of things is barely living at all. Life has depth as well as breadth. We are meant to feel all our emotions—fear and regret as well as joy. We are capable of questioning ourselves for a reason: so we can grow emotionally and spiritually larger.

Am I doing the right thing? Do I try to control others too much? Why do I feel inadequate at work? What's wrong with my relationships? How can I make them better? Without these questions we would not find answers, and the search for answers is what growth is all about. So when we find obstacles in our life, we can now see them as questions, and welcome the opportunity for growth.

Today, let me welcome one obstacle in my life as an opportunity, and listen to the question it asks me.

December 27

*It is better to drink of deep griefs than to
taste shallow pleasures.*

William Hazlitt

When we are in the throes of grief it is hard to
find hope or joy or even to accept support from those
who love us. All we can think of is our loss, our perspective is limited to the memory of lost joys and this
moment of seemingly unendurable sadness. Yet we do
survive grief. We come out of it slowly, as though
waking up and squinting our eyes in the bright sunlight. From experience we know that we have grown
stronger from past grief. We have learned who is able
and willing to support us in tough times. We have
learned to depend on the guidance and care of God. In
short, we have learned that we are not alone, and that
we have inner resources we were unaware of.

Life is bound to bring us grief, just as it brings us
joy. We have already lost our childhood. We will lose
friends, parents, pets, and other loved ones. We will
sometimes see our dreams shattered, only to come
back and build new ones.

Grief tests our faith, hones our prayer, and brings
out the best in our true friends who stand by us. It
brings us closer to ourselves and others and makes
what we still have in our lives more precious. These
are the gifts hidden in our tears. When we accept grief
as openly as we do joy, then we are most deeply alive.

*Today, let me accept my own and others' grief and
keep hope alive.*

*Dance is the only art of which we ourselves
are the stuff of which it is made.*

Ted Shawn

This is the best time of life. We have finished
growing physically, we have gotten over much of our
youthful shyness, we have learned a profession or a
trade or other skills of survival such as cooking, reading, money management, or driving. We have learned
games to enjoy in our spare time. We have learned to
raise children. We have much to celebrate, but many of
us have still not learned how.

The most basic celebration is dance. When we
dance we celebrate our bodies, our ability to move,
and we align ourselves with the basic rhythms of life.
Perhaps we were too shy to learn to dance when we
were young. Perhaps we feel awkward and shy trying
it now. But there is always a way to learn. We can take
lessons, join a folk dancing group, or simply create our
own dances in the privacy of our homes when we are
alone.

The benefits of dancing are many. Exercise,
increasing self-confidence, self-expression, and the
development of our creative spirit are only a few. Most
of all, we experience union with what we are doing,
and this is a joy we all deserve to have today.

*Today, let me take time alone to improvise my own
dance for a few minutes.*

December 29

I prefer old age to the alternative.
  Maurice Chevalier

Now is not the time to moan about how old we're getting. Now is not the time to grieve for our lost youth. Now is the time to celebrate having come this far. We aren't too old to play, or to try new sports or new adventures. We're more able than ever to enjoy relationships. We have perspective on ourselves and the world. We can enjoy quiet moments alone because our lives have deepened over the years, evolving a rich inner vitality comprised of memory, insight, and confidence.

It's true that we're only as old as we feel. It's true that we get better with age. We may not be stronger, more athletic, or as slim as we once were, but we improve where it really counts—inside.

These are important days for us. All the years of primary learning and rehearsal are over. We can feel sure of ourselves even when we take on new challenges because we know what it takes to learn and succeed. We have learned to be human, to succeed at surviving and growing, and we are ready to begin a new growth of the spirit which will never end.

Today, let me be thankful for having come this far.

It is as natural to die as to be born.

Francis Bacon

Death is the inevitable conclusion to all of us. We may not like it, but we know it. We even come to accept it over time. Such acceptance can make our lives more full. It is ironic that, though we can come to the point of accepting the sureness of our own death and the deaths of our loved ones, we have such trouble accepting our own and others' human flaws. Just as death is part of life, failure is part of success, and personality defects are part of the whole person—we would be incomplete without them.

Coming to terms with one aspect of life can often bring us closer to peace of mind in another area. To accept death is to also accept life, and life is imperfect, unpredictable, and often out of our control. The common thread that runs through all this is the presence of a Higher Power, Whose plan includes each of us.

Yes, death is natural. But when we sense the lessons in nature, we see life emerging from death all around us: last year's leaves that fertilize the soil; the butterfly which emerges from the caterpillar; the new strength we gain from facing our pain and sorrow. In accepting our place in nature, we can also sense an elevated place, a spiritual destiny, which knows no bounds, not even death.

Today, let me accept and embrace the life I enjoy in this moment.

December 31

A good man isn't good for everything.
    John W. Gardner

By now we've noticed that we're not perfect. In fact, we may have come to look at ourselves with a jaundiced eye, seeing ourselves as failures because our children aren't perfectly happy or because we aren't a movie actress or president of the company or queen of the hop. But we must have done some things right. Our children did get schooling. We have lived long enough to begin to learn something useful about ourselves. And we still have the time and ability to change, to seek out new challenges, to make new friends, and to accept our own limitations.

Self-acceptance is a key to our happiness. It frees us to love ourselves for what we are doing right, and to forgive ourselves for our mistakes. When we can forget past failures and concentrate on what we are good at, the future is limitless. We have lived this long for a reason—to see that the future is richer than we could ever have imagined, and that we, just as we are, occupy a vital space in the tapestry of life.

Today, let me accept who I am and enjoy my place in the world.

INDEX

Abuse. . . . . .Aug. 12
Acceptance . . . . .Feb. 26; March 8; April 15;
April 30; July 3; Oct. 29;
Nov. 30; Dec. 30
Accepting Love . . . . .June 25
Afterlife. . . . . .Feb. 16
Aging. . . . . .Jan. 4; Feb. 10; March 21;
April 22; May 6; June 6;
Aug. 13; Aug. 25; Sept. 17;
Oct. 18; Oct. 27; Oct. 29;
Nov. 1; Nov. 22; Dec. 19;
Dec. 29
Aging Parents . . . . .Nov. 5
Anger. . . . . .Jan. 11; July 30; Sept. 22;
Nov. 7; Nov. 19; Nov. 21
Answers. . . . . .Feb. 23; Oct. 30
Asking for Help. . . . . .Aug. 11
Assertiveness. . . . . .June 2
Awe .Feb. 2
Beauty . . . . .April 27; May 7
Birth . . . . .Dec. 17
Boredom . . . . .April 12; July 24
Boundaries. . . . . .June 22; Aug. 18
Caretaking. . . . . .July 7
Celebrating Life . . . . .Feb. 8
Celebrating Ourselves . . . . . .June 9
Centering. . . . . .Sept. 19; Sept. 26
Change . . . . .Feb. 4; Feb. 5; March 2;
April 11; April 21; April
24; April 26; May 9; May
25; June 7; Aug. 7; Oct. 2;
Oct. 11; Oct. 17; Oct. 20;
Oct. 21; Nov. 27
Changing Ourselves . . . . .June 22

Children .... March 31; April 17; May
                         13; June 19; July 2; July 7;
                         July 31; Aug. 16; Aug. 30;
                         Nov. 21; Nov. 26; Dec. 5
Choices .... Feb. 7; June 6; July 6
COA..................... April 3
Commitment .... June 26
Communication .... June 11; Nov. 11
Compassion .... May 26; Aug. 30; Sept. 2
Connectedness............ Jan. 9
Conscience .... March 9
Controlling .... July 5; July 15; Dec. 24
Courage.................. Feb. 9; May 17; May 28;
                         Nov. 4
Creativity............... Dec. 15
Dance .... Dec. 28
Dating .... June 10
Daydreams .... Jan. 10
Death.................... Feb. 16; March 19; July 29;
                         Nov. 13; Dec. 30
Decisions................ Feb. 12; July 13;
Depression............... July 12
Detachment .... March 27
Disaster .... March 25
Divorce .... Aug. 21
Dreams .... Feb. 13; Oct. 31; Nov. 29
Dying.................... May 24
Empowerment .... July 6
Empty Nest .... May 13
Energy .... Jan. 14
Enjoying Life............ Feb. 10
Environment .... March 6; April 7; Dec. 8
Exercise................. March 5; Aug. 22; Sept. 5
Experience............... Oct. 14
Expressing Feelings....... June 16
Faith .... April 2; June 14; Nov. 2

Family .Oct. 5
Faults .May 16
Fear . . . . .May 4; Sept. 14; Sept. 23;
                                          Dec. 20
Fear of Death . . . . .June 1
Fear of Failure . . . . .March 4; May 5; Dec. 23
Fellowship . . . . .Jan. 12
Forgiveness . . . . .Feb. 22; March 3; April 3;
                                          July 14; July 22; July 30;
                                          Aug. 9; Dec. 12
Freedom . . . . .April 20; May 8; Sept. 23;
                                          Oct. 23; Oct. 26
Freedom to Choose . . . . .Aug. 17
Friendship . . . . .June 29; Aug. 14; Sept. 29;
                                          Oct. 25
Goals .Feb. 23; March 28; Aug. 26
God . . . . .July 27; Oct. 16
God's Love . . . . .Nov. 18; Dec. 6; Dec. 11
God's Will . . . . .Nov. 9; Nov. 16; Dec. 4
Grace .Nov. 6
Grandchildren . . . . .May 30; July 2
Gratitude . . . . .March 25; April 27; Oct.
                                          27; Dec. 3; Dec. 29
Grief .Jan. 20; March 11; March
                                          14; April 18; May 13; May
                                          24; July 9; July 21; July 29;
                                          Aug. 8; Dec. 27
Guilt .Jan. 17; Feb. 11; Feb. 28;
                                          March 30; Sept. 7; Oct. 4
Happiness . . . . .March 23; July 2; July 3;
                                          Nov. 22
Harmony . . . . .Feb. 25
Healing . . . . .April 6; May 14; July 4;
                                          Aug. 12
Healing Compassion . . . . .Sept. 12

Healthy Love . . . . .Feb. 14; March 29;
                                      April 16; Aug. 17
Hearing Others . . . . .Jan. 3
Higher Choices . . . . .Aug. 10
Higher Power. . . . . .Feb. 18; March 7; March
                                      16; April 4; Aug. 2; Sept.
                                      4; Oct. 16
Higher Power, God . . . . .Jan. 1
Honesty . . . . .Jan. 8; April 10; May 17;
                                      May 25; June 2; June 24;
                                      Sept. 30; Nov. 17
Hope . . . . .Feb. 11; Sept. 3
Humility . . . . .March 24
Humor. . . . . .March 17; May 15; Sept. 9;
                                      Sept. 21; Sept. 24
Illness . . . . .Jan. 6; Feb. 25; April 6
Indifference. . . . . .Nov. 10
Inner Peace . . . . .April 1
Inner Resources. . . . . .Aug. 31
Intimacy . . . . .March 22; May 2; Sept. 1;
                                      Sept. 22
Intuition. . . . . .April 23
Inventory, self . . . . .Sept. 16
Isolation. . . . . .July 10
Joy . . . . .May 8; May 29; Sept. 3;
                                      Oct. 15; Nov. 14; Nov. 25
Kindness . . . . .May 18
Laughter . . . . .March 17; May 15; Sept. 9;
                                      Sept. 21; Sept. 24
Learning from Difficulties . . .May 19; Dec. 23
Legacy. . . . . .July 18
Letting Go. . . . . .Jan. 1; Jan. 24; Feb. 6;
                                      March 3; May 23; July 8;
                                      July 15; Sept. 19; Nov. 4;
                                      Nov. 27
Letting Go of. . . . . .Aug. 16; Aug. 30